O R I G A M I

INSPIRED BY JAPANESE PRINTS

VIKING

First published in 1998 by The Metropolitan Museum of Art, New York,
and Viking, A Division of Penguin Putnam Books for Young Readers, 345 Hudson Street, New York, New York
10014, U.S.A., and Penguin Books Canada, Ltd., 10 Alcorn Avenue, Toronto, Ontario, Canada M4V 3B2

10 9 8 7 6 5 4 3 2

Copyright © 1998 by The Metropolitan Museum of Art
Introduction, instructions, diagrams, and models © 1998 by Steve and Megumi Biddle
All rights reserved
ISBN 0-87099-866-8 MMA
ISBN 0-670-88206-2 Viking

Visit the Museum's Web site: www.metmuseum.org

All works of art are Japanese prints from the collections of The Metropolitan Museum of Art.

Produced by the Department of Special Publications, The Metropolitan Museum of Art.
Publishing Manager, Robie Rogge; Editor, Mary Beth Brewer; Production, Tatiana Ginsberg

Text on the Japanese prints by Donna Welton, Assistant Curator, Department of Asian Art

Photography of the Japanese prints by The Metropolitan Museum of Art Photograph Studio
Photography of the origami models by Les Morsillo

Design by Miriam Berman, with Sophia Stavropoulos

Printed in Hong Kong

O R I G A M I
I N S P I R E D   B Y   J A P A N E S E   P R I N T S

BY
STEVE AND MEGUMI BIDDLE

THE METROPOLITAN MUSEUM OF ART
VIKING

NEW YORK

CONTENTS

44
Butterfly Chōcho

47
Figure Yakko san

49
Basket Kago

51
Wooden Stand Sanbō

54
Chopstick Wrapper
Hashi zutsumi

55
Goldfish Kingyo

57
Japanese Bobtail Cat
Neko

61
Owl Mimizuku

64
Boat Takara bune

67
Flapping Bird
Habataku tori

69
Crane Tsuru

71
Phoenix Hōō

74
Chrysanthemum Kiku

77
Persimmon Kaki

79
Frog Kaeru

82
Iris Ayame

85
Snail Katatsumuri

88
Dragonfly Tonbo

91
Bellflower Kikyō

93
Umbrella Kasa

INTRODUCTION

Welcome to the fabulous world of origami—the art of paper folding. It is a fascinating craft, one that can be enjoyed by anyone, regardless of age, nationality, or language. Each year more and more people are exploring origami, and nowadays people of all ages and from many parts of the world are enjoying folding paper for pleasure.

If you have never tried origami before, this book is an excellent place to begin. The models included range from the simple to the complex, and the text will introduce you to traditional folds, as well as to some that are featured here for the first time. You may find it easiest to work your way through the book from beginning to end, as the more complicated folds build on techniques explained earlier in the book.

Like many traditional books on origami, this one includes models of animals, insects, birds, and flowers. What sets this book apart, however, is their inspiration. Each model is based on a splendid Japanese print from the collections of The Metropolitan Museum of Art, and every print is accompanied with text written by a curator from the Museum discussing the art and the era in which it was created. As you explore the delightful world of paper folding, you will also become acquainted with one of the most intriguing areas of Asian art.

The pocket on the front of this book contains traditional origami paper, colored on one side and white on the other. You can purchase additional packets at stationery shops, Asian gift shops, toy stores, and craft and art supply stores. Part of the fun of origami is choosing what type of paper to fold. The photographs of finished models that appear on the contents pages and that introduce each section of this book suggest the kinds of papers you might eventually try. For papers that have a textured or decorative surface, look in stationery stores and in those that carry art supplies. For beautifully patterned paper, try using gift wrap from stationery stores. There you can

also find opalescent papers and paper-backed metallic foil. Or you can use writing paper, typing paper, computer paper, and even pages cut from a magazine. In fact, all kinds of paper can be used for origami.

Matching the paper to the model is an exciting challenge, and in the finished pieces reproduced in this book you can see what we used from our own collections to make the models look their best. Once you have mastered the basics of paper folding using standard paper, you may be inspired to try working with other types.

Most of the models in this book can be folded from one square of paper, but a few require more. The instructions that introduce each project clearly state what you will need. If you are using your own paper rather than the paper supplied in the pocket on the front of the book, make sure it is cut absolutely square. There is nothing more frustrating than trying to fold a nearly square square!

To learn more about origami, you can contact the following organizations:

Origami USA, 15 West 77th Street, New York, New York 10024-5192

British Origami Society, 35 Corfe Crescent, Hazel Grove, Stockport, Cheshire, SK7 5PR

The Nippon Origami Association, 2-064 Domir Gobancho, 12 Gobancho, Chiyodaku, Tokyo 102-0076

Finally, we would like to echo the words of our very good origami friends, the late Lillian Oppenheimer of New York City and Toshie Takahama of Tokyo, Japan: Always remember that the real secret of origami lies in the giving and sharing with others. We hope you'll have fun discovering the many creative possibilities of origami.

Steve and Megumi Biddle

THE ORIGINS OF ORIGAMI

The development of paper folding in the West can be traced back to a company of Japanese jugglers who visited Europe in the 1860s, at the time when the Japanese were beginning to make contact with other cultures. The jugglers brought with them the method for folding the "flapping bird." Soon directions for this and other folds were appearing in various European publications. Magicians, including Harry Houdini, were especially interested in paper folding, attesting to the association between origami and magic, which continues today.

Paper folding, of course, had begun long before— in fact nearly two thousand years before, with the invention of paper in China in 105 A.D. Paper documents were usually rolled and their ends tied. There is a long tradition in China of folding paper into decorative shapes that are tossed onto coffins as symbols of objects for the departed to take with them into the next world.

For more than five hundred years, the Chinese kept the paper-making process a secret. Then in the eighth century, Chinese invaders captured in Arabia were forced to reveal the technique. Eventually the process reached southern Europe.

Documents show that the Spanish symbol of paper folding, the *pajarita,* or "little bird," existed in the seventeenth century. Elsewhere in Europe, the art of paper folding was echoed in decorative napkin folds. At a banquet given by the sixteenth-century pope Gregory XIII, the setting included a table "decorated with wonderfully folded napkins." And the English diarist Samuel Pepys wrote in March 1668, "Thence home and there find one laying napkins against tomorrow in figures of all sorts."

The Japanese tradition of folding paper is a long and continuous one. It probably began in the sixth century, when a Buddhist priest brought paper-making methods to Japan from China by way of Korea. At that time, paper was a rare and precious commodity, and a formal kind of paper folding developed for use in both religious and secular life. There is perhaps another reason for the importance of paper in Japanese life. The Japanese word *kami* can mean "paper" as well as "God," even though they are written differently. This has given rise to a belief that paper is sacred. It has long been associated with the Shinto religion and the folding of human figures *(hitogata)* that are blessed by God.

During Japan's Edo period (1600–1868), a time of development in the arts, paper became inexpensive enough to be used by everyone, and origami became a form of entertainment. Japanese woodblock prints from this period show origami models, people folding paper, and origami in kimono patterns. Two such prints are reproduced in the opening pages of this book.

In the 1890s, the Japanese government introduced a widespread system of preschool education, and origami was introduced as a tool for bringing minds and hands into coordination. It is still taught to young children today.

Since the 1950s, interest in origami has proliferated in the United States and Great Britain as well as Japan, resulting in a variety of books and articles on the subject and in the founding of many origami societies worldwide. The addresses of three of the most important societies are given on page 7.

Despite its popularity, for many years origami generated only a dozen or so noteworthy creations, such as the flapping bird and jumping frog, both of which are included in this book. Today, however, it seems there is no shape that cannot be folded. And, as you will discover when you fold the projects in this book, it can be tremendously exciting to see a flat piece of paper become transformed into a three-dimensional object. Learning how to fold new models is thrilling: Enjoy the ones you encounter in these pages.

HELPFUL TIPS

Before you try any of the projects in this book, here are some helpful tips that will make origami easier:

- Before you start, make sure your paper is the correct shape.

- Fold on a smooth, flat surface, such as a table or a book. Make your folds neat and accurate.

- Press your folds into place by running your thumbnail along them. Do not panic if your first few attempts at folding are not very successful. With practice you will come to understand the ways a piece of paper behaves when it is folded.

- In the diagrams in this book, the shading represents the colored side of the paper.

- Look at each diagram carefully, read the instructions, then look ahead to the next diagram to see what shape should be created when you have completed the step you are working on

- You will find it easiest to work your way through from the beginning of this book to the end, as some of the folding projects and procedures in later sections are based partially on previous ones. However, if you are an experienced paperfolder and can follow origami instructions without too much help, you can, of course, select any design as a starting point.

- Above all, if a fold or whole model does not work out, do not give up hope. Go through all the illustrations one by one, checking that you have read the instructions correctly and have not missed an important word or overlooked a symbol. If you are still unable to complete the model, put it to one side and come back to it another day with a fresh mind.

SYMBOLS AND BASIC FOLDING PROCEDURES

The symbols used in this book were developed by the Nippon Origami Association, and they show the direction in which paper should be folded. Look at the diagrams very carefully to see which way the dashes, dots, and arrows go over, through, and under the paper, and fold your paper accordingly.

If you are new to origami, we suggest that you take a few squares of paper and study the following symbols and folding procedures before trying any of the origami projects. After spending a few minutes learning the drawings, you will be able to follow the illustrations in almost any origami book, even if you cannot understand the language in which it is written.

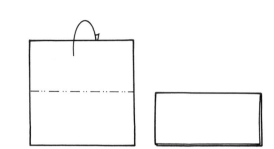

Mountain fold (fold behind)

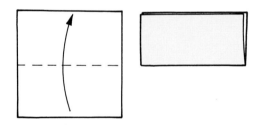

Valley fold (fold in front)

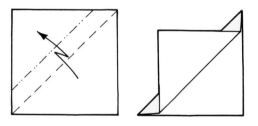

Step fold

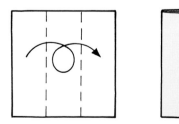

Fold over and over

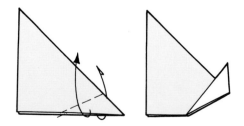

Outside reverse fold

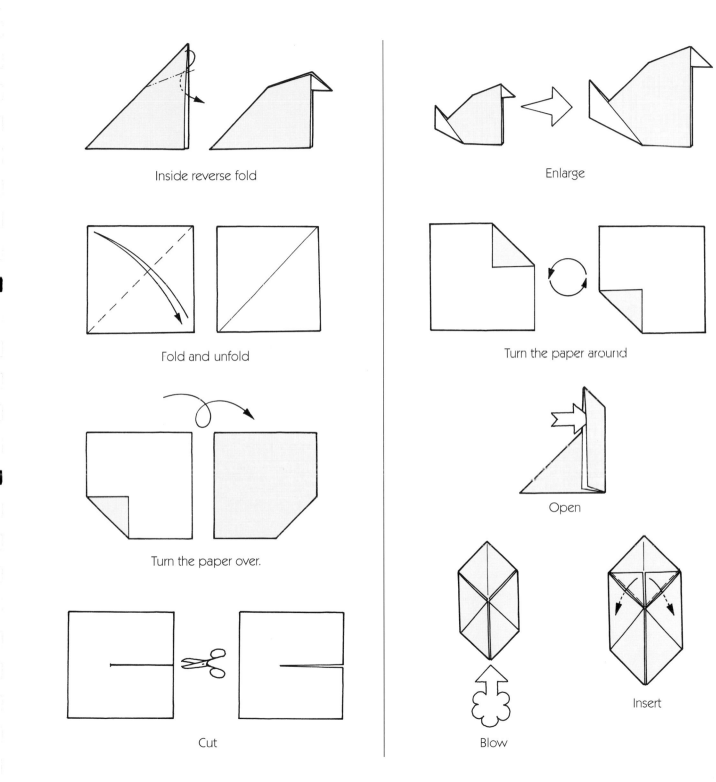

Inside reverse fold

Enlarge

Fold and unfold

Turn the paper around

Turn the paper over.

Open

Cut

Blow

Insert

11

Cup Koppu

In Japan, green tea is served in cups without handles. Drinking it warms the hands as well as the body. During the artist Utamaro's era, teahouses were places both for travelers to rest and for neighbors to pass the time in conversation with friends and with lovely young waitresses.

The waitress Okita worked at a teahouse in Naniwacho. She was famous for her beauty, and she would have been immediately recognized in this print. Since at the time women could be specifically identified in prints only if they were professional entertainers, Utamaro and his publisher could not include Okita's name. Instead, they used a poem to let people know indirectly that the woman pictured was Okita:

Naniwacho chaya ni yasuraide–
Naniwazu no na ni ou mono wa
yuki kai ni ashi no tomaranu hito mo
araji na

Written while relaxing at a teahouse in
    Naniwacho–
No one can fail to stop in here
as they pass by the leggy weeds
    of Naniwa's straits
whatever their reason for coming.

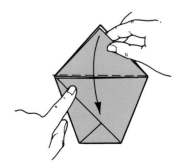

To make a diaper fold, fold a square piece of paper in half along its diagonal. In Japan, this is called a shawl fold or a triangle fold.

Use a square piece of paper, white side up.

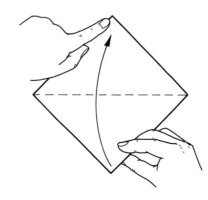

1 Turn the square around to look like a diamond. Valley fold it in half from bottom to top to make . . .

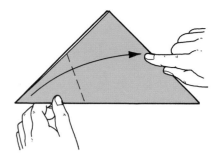

2 a diaper fold. Valley fold the bottom left-hand point over to meet the opposite side.

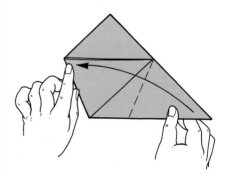

3 Valley fold the bottom right-hand point over to meet the opposite side.

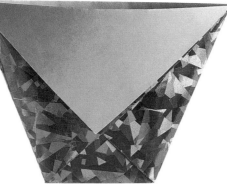

4 Valley fold the top point down.

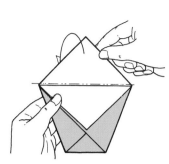

5 Mountain fold the remaining top point behind.

6 To complete the cup, slightly open the paper out along its top edge.

Okita, of the Naniwaya Tea Shop
Kitagawa Utamaro, Japanese, 1753–1806
Polychrome woodblock print, 14⅞ x 9⅞ in., ca. 1794
H. O. Havemeyer Collection, Bequest of
Mrs. H. O. Havemeyer, 1929   JP1668

Mount Fuji Fuji san

Edo is an earlier name for the city of Tokyo. In the nineteenth century, the almost surreal beauty of the dormant volcano Fuji dominated Edo's skyline, and even today the mountain looms up on clear days. Fuji is a sacred mountain; many devotees make a pilgrimage there, climbing its slopes to view the sunrise at least once. The artist Hokusai caught the many changing moods of Fuji in his series of prints, *Thirty-six Views of Mount Fuji*, sensitively capturing the atmosphere and the seasons.

South Wind, Clear Sky
Katsushika Hokusai, Japanese, 1760–1849
Polychrome woodblock print from the series
Thirty-six Views of Mount Fuji (Fugaku Sanjūrokkei), 9⅞ x 14 in., ca. 1831
Rogers Fund, 1914   JP9

14

This charming model makes an ideal place card for a party.

Use a square piece of paper, colored side up.

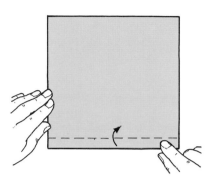

1 Valley fold a little of the bottom edge over.

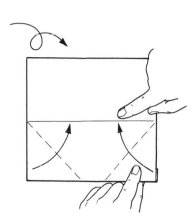

3 Turn the paper over. Valley fold the bottom corners up to meet the middle fold line.

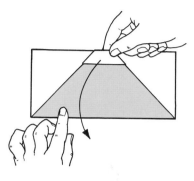

5 To complete, lift the front flap of paper outward, so that . . .

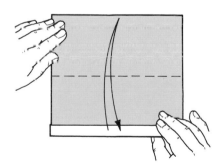

2 Fold and unfold the paper in half from bottom to top.

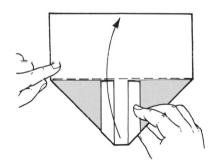

4 Valley fold the paper in half from bottom to top.

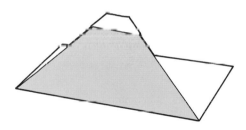

6 Mount Fuji will sit up when placed on a flat surface.

Fan Sensu

In old Japan, fans were used as props in dances as well as in more personal dramas. They were often decorated by famous artists, and the format inspired many innovative paintings. Later, they were sometimes removed from their bamboo ribs and framed, pasted on screens for decoration, or collected in albums. This print is a parody: It shows women as if they were merchants running a fan shop. The customers have replaced the shop's owners!

The Eijudo Fan Shop
Utagawa Toyokuni, Japanese, 1769–1825
Triptych of polychrome woodblock prints, each 15⅛ x 10⅛ in.
The Howard Mansfield Collection,
Purchase, Rogers Fund, 1936   JP2725

This is a very simple way to make a fan. It will look especially beautiful when it is made from a square of colorful wrapping paper.

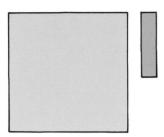

Use a square piece of paper, white side up. You will also need a tube of glue and a small rectangular piece of paper.

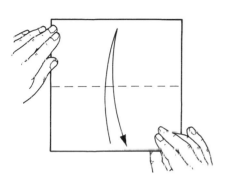

1 Fold and unfold the square in half from bottom to top.

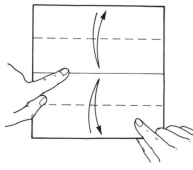

2 Fold and unfold the top and bottom edges as shown.

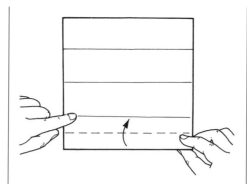

3 Valley fold the bottom edge up to meet the adjacent fold line.

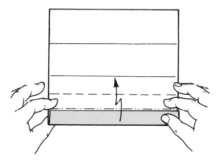

4 From the bottom, pleat the paper into equal sections by mountain and valley folding.

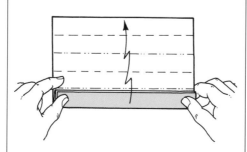

5 Note that the mountain folds take place along existing fold lines.

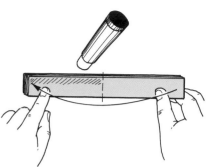

6 Valley fold the paper in half from side to side and glue the two halves together.

7 Form the handle by gluing the small rectangular piece of paper around the folded end as shown.

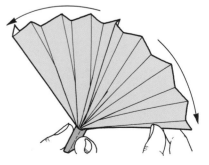

8 To complete the fan, open out the pleats.

Bamboo Letterfold Takenoko zutsumi

In China, Korea, and Japan, people celebrate the *Twenty-four Paragons of Filial Piety*, tales of extraordinary acts done to help parents. In one story, Meng Zong went out in the dead of winter to search for bamboo shoots, which his aged mother craved. To reward his devotion, several shoots miraculously sprang up through the snow. This print by the artist Harunobu shows a young woman acting out the part of Meng Zong.

Mōsō
(Meng Zong Digging Bamboo
Shoots for His Mother in Snow)
Suzuki Harunobu,
Japanese, 1725–1770
Polychrome woodblock print
from the series *Twenty-four
Paragons of Filial Piety*,
11⅛ x 8¾ in., ca. 1765
The Howard Mansfield Collection,
Purchase, Rogers Fund, 1936
JP2439

Here is a novel way of folding a letter.

Use a rectangular piece of paper, white or written side up.

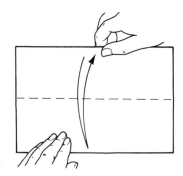

1 Place the rectangle sideways. Fold and unfold it in half from top to bottom.

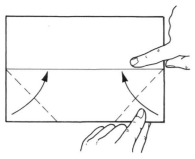

2 Valley fold the bottom corners up to meet the middle fold line.

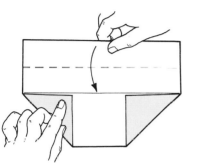

3 Valley fold the top edge down to meet the middle fold line.

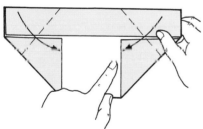

4 Valley fold the top corners down to meet the vertical edges as shown.

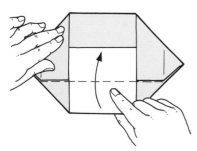

5 Valley fold the bottom edge up to meet the horizontal edge.

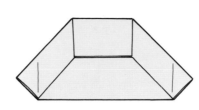

6 This should be the result.

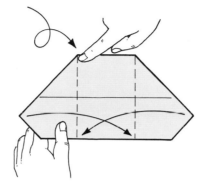

7 Turn the paper over. Valley fold the left-hand corner over as shown. Repeat with the right-hand corner, and . . .

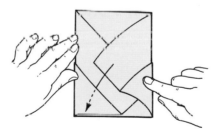

8 tuck it underneath the opposite sloping edge.

9 This should be the result.

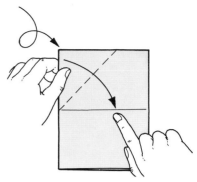

10 Turn the paper over. Valley fold the top left-hand corner down to meet the horizontal fold line.

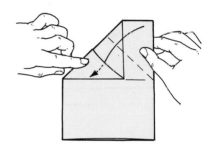

11 Valley fold the top right-hand corner down, and tuck it underneath the opposite sloping edge as shown.

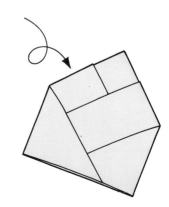

12 To complete the bamboo letterfold, turn the paper over.

Dove Hato

A passage from the eighth-century chronicle the *Kojiki* describes the mournful sound of the dove like this:

Hasa no yama no hato no shitanaki ni nauku.

I weep with the murmuring sound of doves crying at Mount Hasa.

Rock Doves and Tree Sparrows
Kitagawa Utamaro, Japanese, 1753–1806
Polychrome woodblock print from the illustrated book *A Chorus of Birds* (*Momo-chidori*), 9⅜ x 14⅛ in., ca. 1790
H. O. Havemeyer Collection, Bequest of Mrs. H. O. Havemeyer, 1929
Japanese Book No. 77, vol. II, folio 4

Try changing the angle of the head and wings each time you fold this model to see how many different doves you can create.

Use a square piece of paper, white side up.

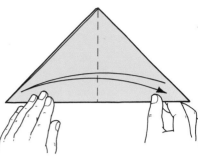

1 Begin with a diaper fold (see page 12). Fold and unfold it in half from side to side.

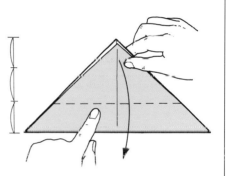

2 Valley fold the top points down two-thirds of the way as shown.

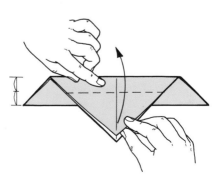

3 Valley fold the front flap of paper up as shown.

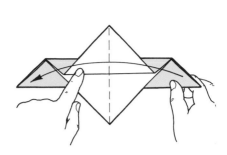

4 To make the wings, valley fold the paper in half from right to left.

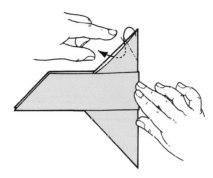

5 Now inside reverse fold the top point. This is what you do:

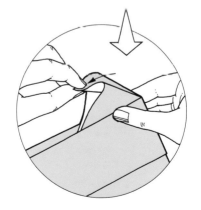

6 Place your thumb into the point's groove and, with your forefinger on top, pull the point down inside itself. To make the head and beak, press the paper flat.

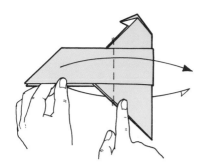

7 Valley fold the front wing over as shown. Repeat behind.

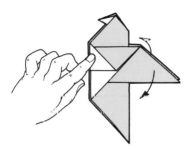

8 Open out the wings slightly.

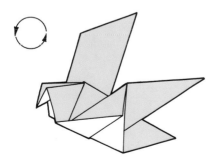

9 To complete the dove, turn the paper around.

LanternChōchin

Hand-held lanterns lit the way to many nighttime parties and lovers' trysts in eighteenth- and nineteenth-century Japan. These lanterns, called *chōchin* in Japanese, were made of lacquered wood and paper. They came in many different forms, and they often advertised restaurants or other well-known buildings in the entertainment district. Utamaro was a master at capturing the casual poses and unguarded moments of the women who worked in such places.

Fashionable Women on an Evening Stroll
Kitagawa Utamaro, Japanese, 1753–1806
Polychrome woodblock print, 20⅛ x 7⁷⁄₁₆ in.
H. O. Havemeyer Collection, Bequest of Mrs. H. O. Havemeyer, 1929   JP1664

This delightful model makes an ideal party decoration.

Use a square piece of paper, white side up.

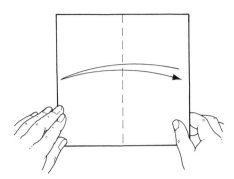

1 Fold and unfold the square in half from side to side.

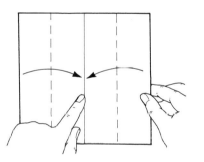

2 Valley fold the sides over to meet the middle fold line.

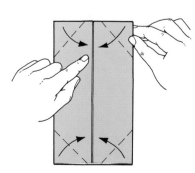

3 Valley fold the top and bottom corners over and towards the middle edges.

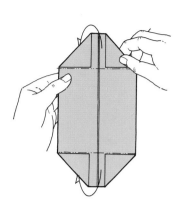

4 Mountain fold the top and bottom points behind as shown.

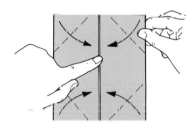

5 Repeat step 3.

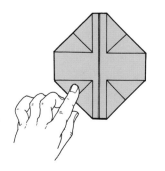

6 This should be the result.

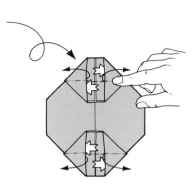

7 Turn the paper over. Carefully open out the pockets of paper. Press them down neatly . . .

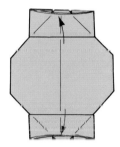

8 into rectangles, so completing the lantern.

Shell Kai

In Japanese art, poems and pictures are sometimes combined, creating a lovely effect. This still life of shells and a plant paired with a porcelain lidded bowl is set off by the lines of a 31-syllable poem known as a *waka*.

Kurenai no
ume irokoki
akagai ni
midori no medatsu
oko no aoyagi.

The deep red
color of the plum blossom
found in the ark shell
pairs with the striking green
of the shell at its side.

A Bowl with Black Shells and an Udo Plant
Japanese, 18th–19th century
New Year card, *surimono* woodblock print
H. O. Havemeyer Collection, Bequest of
Mrs. H. O. Havemeyer, 1929   JP2182

くれなゐの
梅よ色ふき
あかり貝に
みとりのめたつ
をこの青柳

二鐘亭

When you make this model, use pink or cream-colored paper, or a special piece of pearly iridescent paper. The right color and texture will make your finished shell look beautiful and realistic.

Use a square piece of paper, white side up.

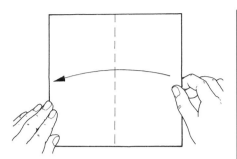

1 Valley fold the square in half from side to side.

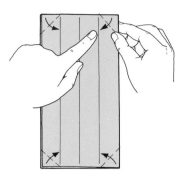

4 Valley fold the corners over to meet their adjacent fold lines.

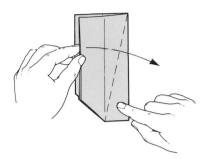

7 Valley fold the front flap of paper as shown.

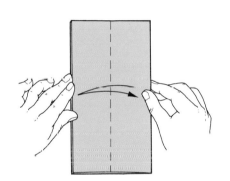

2 Fold and unfold the paper in half from side to side.

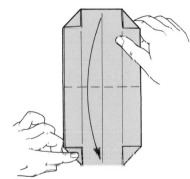

5 Valley fold the paper in half from top to bottom.

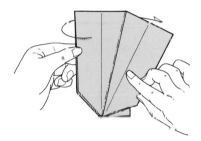

8 Mountain fold the back flap of paper as shown.

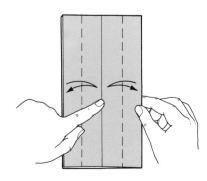

3 Fold and unfold the sides as shown.

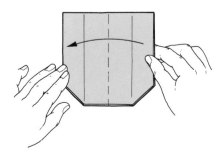

6 Valley fold the paper in half from right to left.

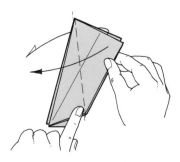

9 Valley fold the front flap of paper as shown. Repeat behind.

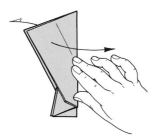

10 Open out the paper.

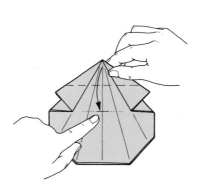

13 Valley fold the top point down as shown.

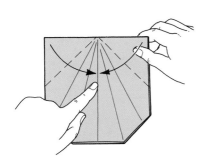

11 Valley fold the top corners down to meet the middle fold line.

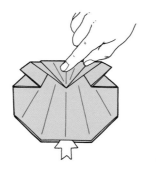

14 Slightly open the paper out along its bottom edge, and shape the shell into place.

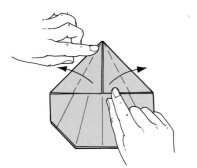

12 Valley fold the middle corners out along the line of the existing fold line underneath.

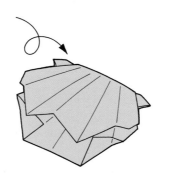

15 To complete the shell, turn the paper over.

Turtle
Kame

On the fifteenth day of the eighth month of the lunar calendar, many temples and shrines have a ceremony, the *Hojo-e,* in which creatures, usually birds or turtles, are released. Many shops and street stalls sell the animals, and purchasers set them free to accumulate merit for their compassion. Hiroshige boldly focuses on a turtle hung on the Mannen Bridge in Fukagawa, which is near the famous Hachiman Shrine. His dramatic composition captures the flavor of this part of old Tokyo: It is one of the finest prints in his series *One Hundred Famous Views of Edo.*

The Mannen-bashi Bridge at Fukagawa
(The Bridge of Ten Thousand Years)
Utagawa Hiroshige, Japanese, 1797–1858
Polychrome woodblock print from the series
One Hundred Famous Views of Edo (Meisho Edo Hyakkei),
14⅛ x 9⁵⁄₁₆ in., 1858
Rogers Fund, 1919   JP1184

Many of the traditional Japanese models have a symbolic meaning. This fold is no exception, as the turtle symbolizes long life.

Use a square piece of paper, white side up. You will also need a pair of scissors.

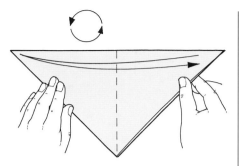

1 Begin with a diaper fold (see page 12). Turn the fold around so it points toward you. Fold and unfold it in half from side to side.

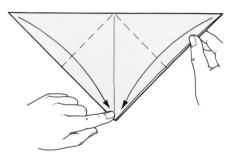

2 Valley fold the top points down to meet the bottom point.

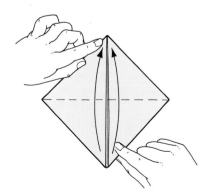

3 Valley fold the bottom points up to meet the top point; you are making the front flippers.

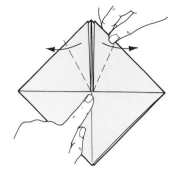

4 Valley fold the flippers out from the middle as shown.

5 From the bottom point, cut along the indicated line to make the back flippers.

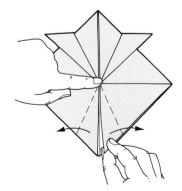

6 Repeat step 4 with the back flippers.

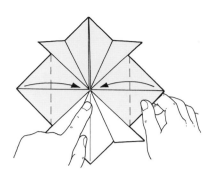

7 Valley fold the side points in toward the middle.

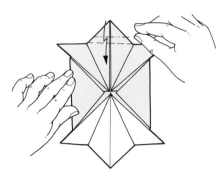

8 Pleat the top point with a valley and a mountain fold, to make the head.

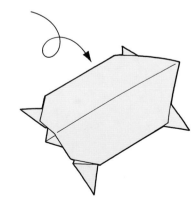

9 To complete the turtle, turn the paper over.

Coat
Happi

Kimono
Kimono

After Japan became a constitutional monarchy in the nineteenth century, an effort was made both publicly and privately to transform the country into a progressive, modern nation. Some thought that Japan should give up its Asian ways and become Western, like Europe and the United States. There were arguments about what should be taught, what houses and government buildings should look like, how people should wear their hair, even what they should eat, and, of course, how people should dress. These prints make fun of that debate by showing how people resemble paper dolls: They can be dressed as anything government or social leaders require.

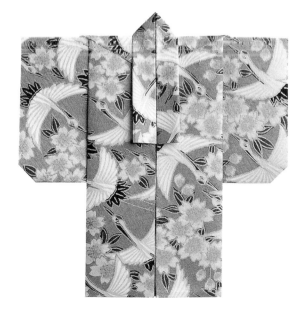

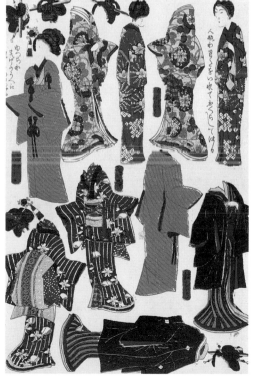

Cut-out Paper Dolls with Clothing
Unknown Japanese artist, 19th century
Woodblock print, 15 x 9⅛ in., 1897–98 *(above left)*
Woodblock print, 14¾ x 9⅛ in., 1897–98 *(above right)*
Gift of Lincoln Kirstein, 1960   JP3381

Coat Happi

Fold this model very carefully! If you aren't accurate, your finished coat won't look neat and tidy.

Use a rectangular piece of paper, 3 x 1 in proportion (for example, 3 x 9 in., or 7.5 x 22.5 cm), colored side up.

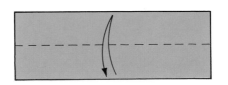

1 Place the rectangle sideways. Fold and unfold it in half from bottom to top.

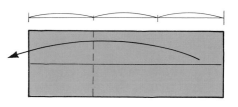

2 Valley fold the right-hand side over two-thirds of the way as shown.

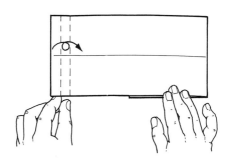

3 Valley fold a little of the left-hand side over and then over again.

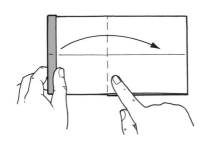

4 Valley fold the left-hand side over along the line of the edge behind to make a flap.

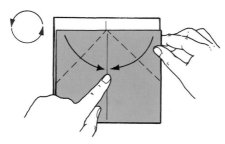

5 Turn the paper around. Valley fold the flap's top corners down to meet the middle fold line to make the collar.

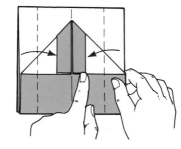

6 Valley fold the right- and left-hand sides over to meet the collar.

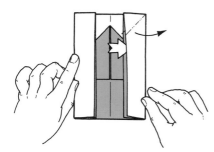

7 Open out the right-hand side and press down its top into the shape of a triangular roof.

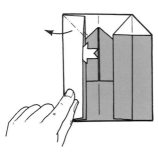

8 Repeat step 7 with the left-hand side.

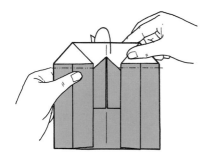

9 Mountain fold the top edge behind as shown.

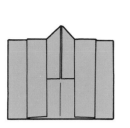

10 This should be the result.

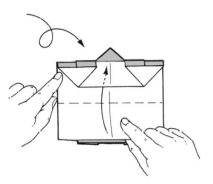

11 Turn the paper over. Valley fold the bottom edge up, at the same time . . .

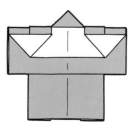

12 tucking it underneath the top layers of paper to make the sleeves.

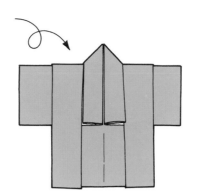

13 To complete the coat, turn the paper over.

KimonoKimono

This model makes an ideal decoration for a piece of notepaper or personal stationery. It is based on the coat.

Use a rectangular piece of paper, 4 x 1 in proportion (for example, 3 x 12 in., or 7.5 x 30 cm), the same color on both sides.

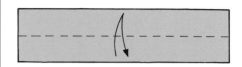

1 Begin by repeating steps 1 to 5 of the coat (see page 30).

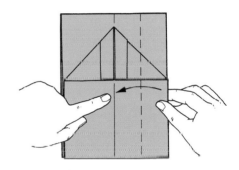

2 Valley fold the right-hand side over to meet the middle fold line.

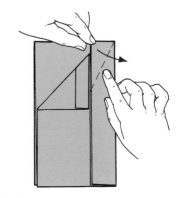

3 Valley fold the side's top edge out on a slant as shown.

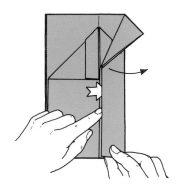

4 Open out the side's top layer of paper and . . .

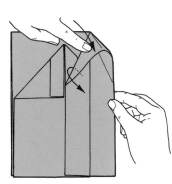

5 press it down as shown. At the same time, tuck the side's slanted edge underneath the collar.

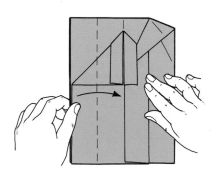

6 Repeat steps 2 to 5 with the left-hand side.

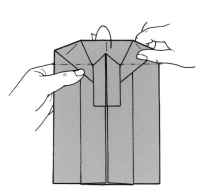

7 Mountain fold the top edge behind.

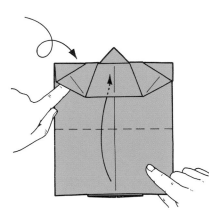

8 Turn the paper over. Valley fold the bottom edge up, at the same time tucking it underneath the top layers of paper.

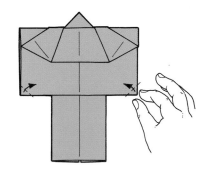

9 Shape the sleeves with valley folds as shown.

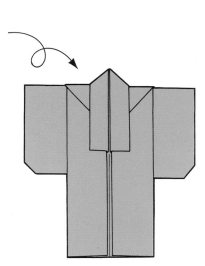

10 To complete the kimono, turn the paper over.

Fish Sakana · **Shrimp** Ebi

So much of Japan is surrounded by the
sea that the water, shore, and sea life
are threaded through the country's
culture, from poetry to prints. Hiroshige's
still-life print is both lovely and amusing.
The artist completed a series of these
compositions called *All Kinds of Fish*
(Sakana Zukushi) in the 1830s.

Horse Mackerel and Shrimp
Utagawa Hiroshige, Japanese, 1797–1858
Polychrome woodblock print from the series *All Kinds of Fish*
(Sakana Zukushi), 10⅛ x 14½ in., 1832–33
Gift of Mr. and Mrs. Bryan Holme, 1980   JP3595

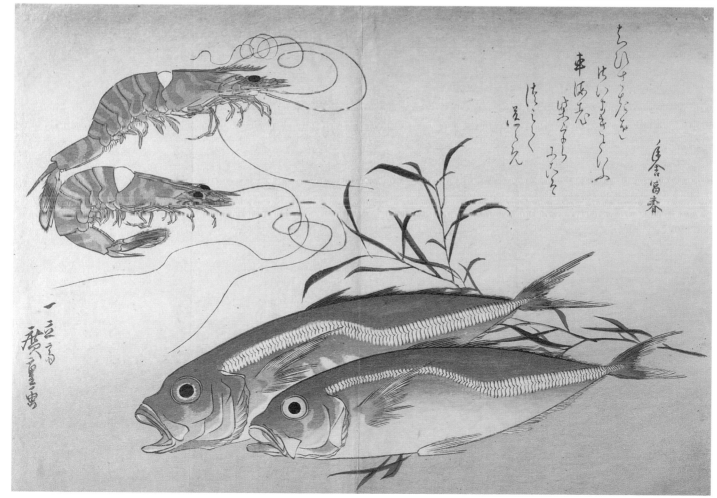

33

Fish Sakana

The kite base, which is named for its shape, forms the foundation of this fish model. As you form the base, make sure you fold accurately.

Use a square piece of paper, white side up.

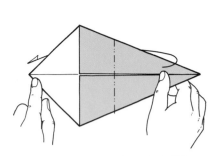

3 Mountain fold the kite base in half from right to left.

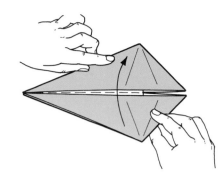

6 along the middle fold line, making a fish base. Valley fold it in half from bottom to top.

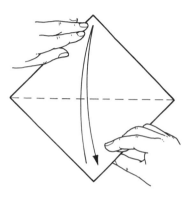

1 Turn the square around to look like a diamond. Fold and unfold it in half from bottom to top.

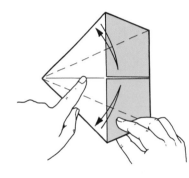

4 From the left-hand corner, fold and unfold the sloping edges as shown.

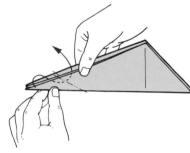

7 Treating the left-hand points as if they were one, inside reverse fold them upward.

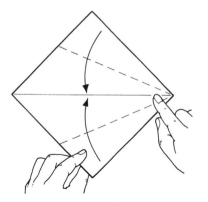

2 From the right-hand corner, valley fold the sloping edges over, so they lie along the middle fold line. Press them flat, making a kite base.

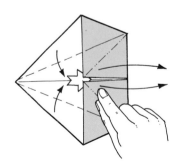

5 Along the existing fold lines, pull the top and bottom flaps of paper over to the right, making their sloping edges come to lie . . .

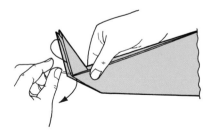

8 Inside reverse fold the inner left-hand point downward to make . . .

9 the tail.

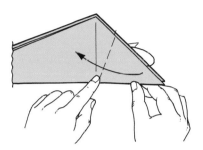

10 Valley fold the right-hand point over as shown to make a front fin. Repeat behind.

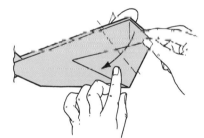

11 Valley fold the right-hand layer of paper over on a slant. Repeat behind.

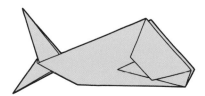

12 Here is the completed fish.

ShrimpEbi

Once you have perfected folding this model, try making it out of shiny metallic foil, which will help the shrimp hold its shape perfectly.

Use a square piece of paper, white side up.

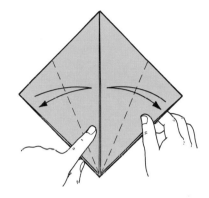

1 Begin by repeating steps 1 and 2 of the turtle (see page 28). Fold and unfold the lower sloping edges as shown.

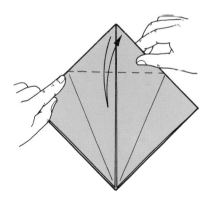

2 Fold and unfold the top point as shown.

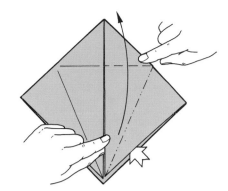

3 Now make a petal fold. This is what you do: Pinch and lift up a bottom point.

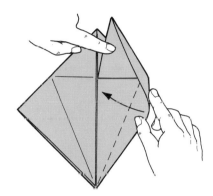

4 Continue to lift up the point, so

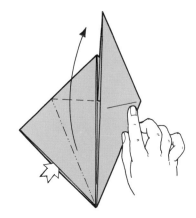

5 its edges meet in the middle. Press the paper flat. Repeat steps 3 to 5 with the remaining bottom point.

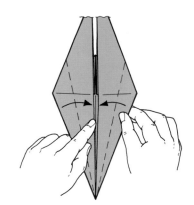

6 Valley fold the lower sloping edges over, so they lie along the middle line, making the body and tail.

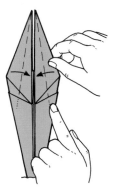

7 To make the antennae, repeat step 6 with the upper sloping edges.

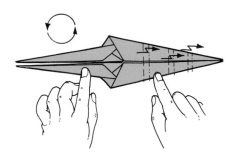

8 Turn the paper around. Pleat the body with a series of step folds.

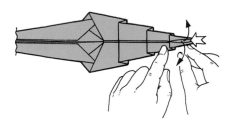

9 Carefully open the right-hand point out.

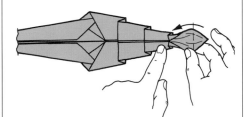

10 To shape the tail, valley fold the point's tip over.

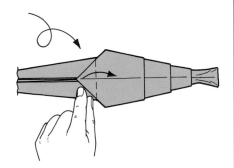

11 Turn the paper over. Valley fold the body's left-hand point over toward the right.

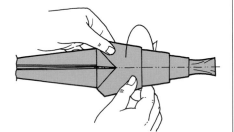

12 Mountain fold the paper in half from top to bottom.

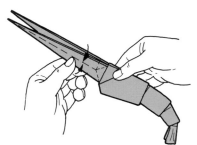

13 Pull the pleats out slightly to curve the body as shown in step 14.

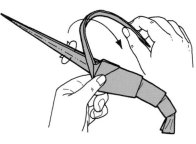

14 Pinch an antenna's sloping sides together, while at the same time . . .

15 curving it backward toward the body. Repeat steps 14 and 15 with the remaining antenna.

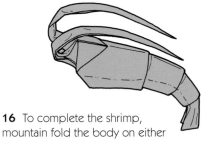

16 To complete the shrimp, mountain fold the body on either side as shown.

Lion Dance Shishi mai

The *shishi mai*, or lion dance, is a favorite street activity celebrating the New Year. Originally it was a dance brought to Japan from Tang Dynasty China (618–907) and performed at court. Later it became a Noh theater dance and was also performed as a religious dance to drive away evil spirits and invoke bountiful grain harvests.

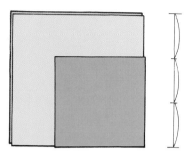

The Lion Dance
Kitagawa Utamaro, Japanese, 1753–1806
Polychrome woodblock print from the illustrated book *Comic Poems on New Year's Customs (Waka Ebisu)*
8¼ x 14¼ in., 1786
Gift of Estate of Samuel Isham, 1914 JP961

This model is made up of similar units, so be very careful not to mix up your paper and the steps. Use three squares of paper, all the same size. You will also need a pair of scissors and a tube of glue.

1 Begin by cutting out a square of paper to the size shown, two-thirds the size of the other pieces. You will use this small square to fold the lion mask.

Lion Mask

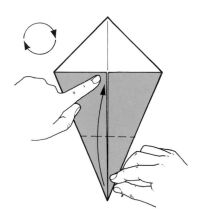

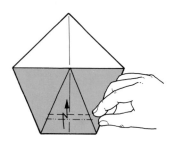

2 Begin by folding the small square into a kite base (see page 34). Turn it around. Valley fold the bottom point up to meet the middle corners as shown.

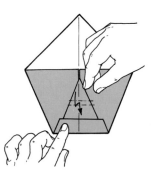

3 To make the mouth, step fold the point.

4 Now step fold the point again to make the nose.

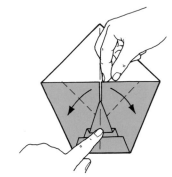

5 Valley fold the two middle corners out and . . .

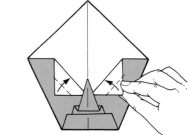

6 back in to make the eyes.

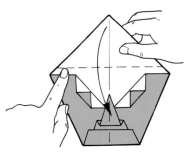

7 Valley fold the top point down as shown to make the forehead.

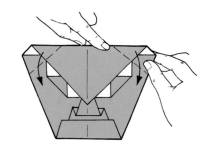

8 Valley fold the sloping sides over to make the ears.

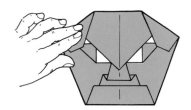

9 This should be the result.

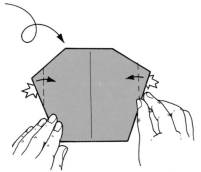

10 Turn the paper over. Valley fold both sloping sides over, while at the same time . . .

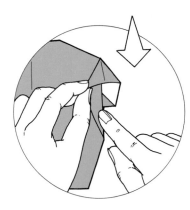

11 pressing their triangular side pockets down neatly.

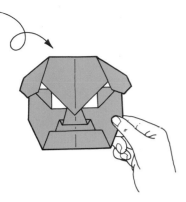

12 To complete the lion mask, turn the paper over.

Legs

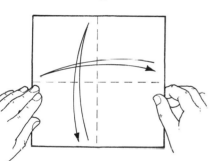

13 Take a square piece of paper and valley fold the opposite sides and top and bottom edges together to mark the vertical and horizontal fold lines, then open the square up again.

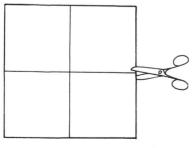

14 Cut along the fold lines to make four small squares.

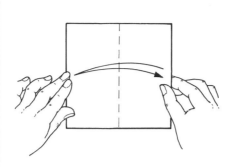

15 Fold and unfold one small square in half from side to side, with the white side on top.

16 Valley fold the sides over to meet the middle fold line.

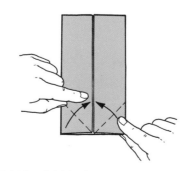

17 Valley fold the bottom corners up to meet the middle edges.

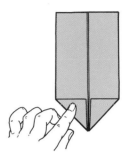

18 This should be the result.

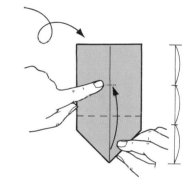

19 Turn the paper over. Valley fold the bottom point up one-third of the way as shown.

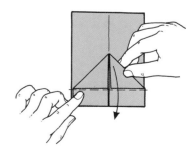

20 Valley fold the point back down to make a pleat in the paper.

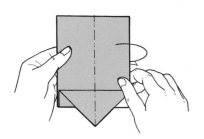

21 Mountain fold the paper in half from right to left.

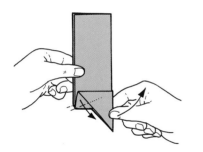

22 Hold the paper as shown and pull the bottom section of paper up . . .

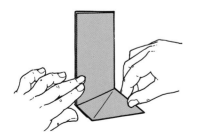

23 as far as the pleat will allow you; you are completing a leg. Repeat steps 15 to 23 with the remaining three small squares.

Body/Assembly

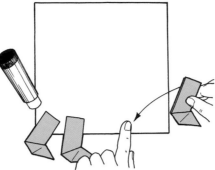

24 Place the third piece of paper before you, with the white side on top, and glue the legs on to it at the desired angles.

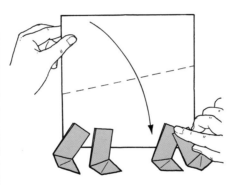

25 Valley fold the square's top edge down on a slant, covering the legs slightly.

26 Valley fold the top left-hand point down on a slant as shown.

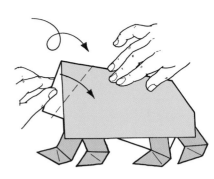

27 Turn the paper over. Repeat step 26.

28 Glue the mask on to the body at the desired angle.

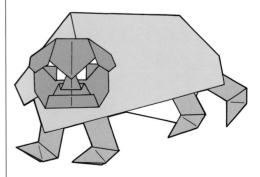

29 Here is the completed lion dance.

Morning Glory
Asagao

Morning glories, or *asagao* ("morning faces"), are a popular summertime plant. Flowers are beloved in Japan for their beauty, and even more for the short-lived nature of their loveliness. That they are such fleeting pleasures makes them all the more precious and poignant.

Morning Glories and Cricket
Utagawa Hiroshige, Japanese, 1797–1858
Polychrome woodblock print from the series *Birds and Flowers (Kacho)*,
13 x 4⅜ in., ca. 1847
The Howard Mansfield Collection,
Purchase, Rogers Fund, 1936   JP2534

Making this morning glory model begins with what is known as the preliminary fold, so called because it is the foundation for several bases and therefore an infinite number of models. In Japan, it's known as the square base. Use two squares of paper, both the same size. You will also need a pair of scissors.

Morning Glory

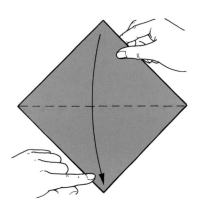

1 Turn one square around to look like a diamond, with the colored side up. Valley fold it in half from top to bottom.

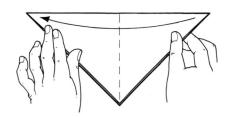

2 Valley fold the paper in half from right to left.

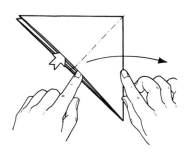

3 Lift the top half up along the middle fold line. Open out the paper and . . .

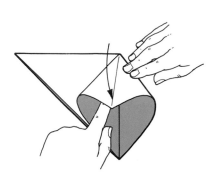

4 press it down neatly . . .

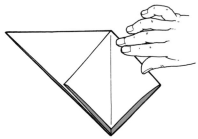

5 into a diamond.

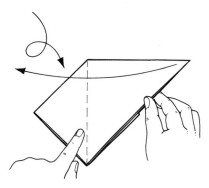

6 Turn the paper over. Repeat steps 2 to 5 to make a preliminary fold.

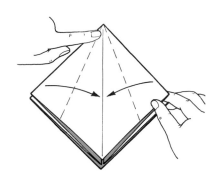

7 Valley fold the upper (folded) sloping edges over, so . . .

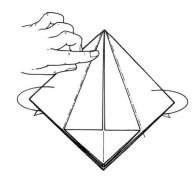

8 they lie along the middle fold line. Repeat behind.

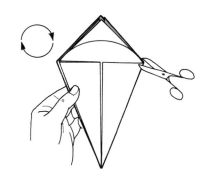

9 Turn the paper around. Cut an arc along the indicated line.

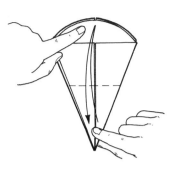

10 Fold and unfold the paper in half from bottom to top.

11 Peel back the top layer of paper as shown to make . . .

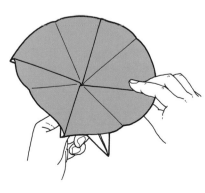

12 the morning glory blossom.

Leaf

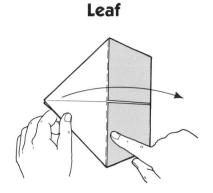

13 With the remaining square piece of paper, repeat steps 1 to 3 of the fish (see page 34). Valley fold the left-hand corner over on a line between the top and bottom points.

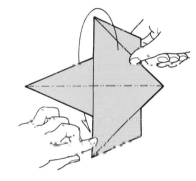

14 Mountain fold the paper in half from top to bottom.

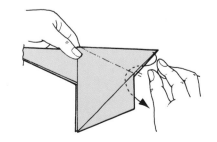

15 Inside reverse fold the right-hand point, and the underneath layer of paper. (See step 16.)

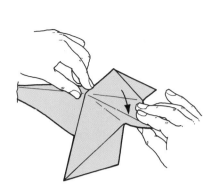

16 This shows step 15 taking place.

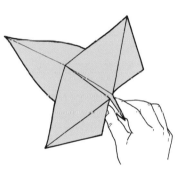

17 To complete the leaf, open out the paper slightly.

18 Display the leaf and morning glory together.

Butterfly Chōcho

In Japanese art, each part of the year is represented by its own particular flora and fauna. Butterflies and poppies appear in the summer, and Utamaro's prints seem to shimmer with the heat of July and August.

Butterflies and Dragonfly in Poppies
Kitagawa Utamaro, Japanese, 1753–1806
Polychrome woodblock prints from the illustrated book
Book of Insects (Ehon Mushi Erabi),
each 10⅛ x 7¼ in., 1788
Rogers Fund, 1918 JP1046

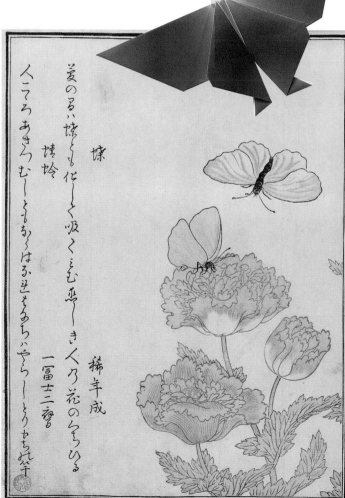

The waterbomb base is so called because it is the starting point for the traditional waterbomb. In Japan it's known as the balloon base.

Use a square piece of paper, white side up.

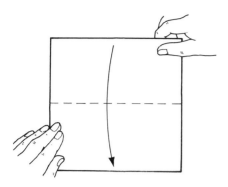

1 Valley fold the square in half from top to bottom.

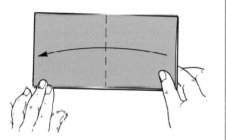

2 Valley fold the paper in half from right to left.

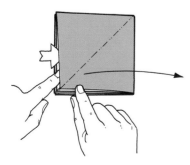

3 Lift the top half up along the middle fold line. Start . . .

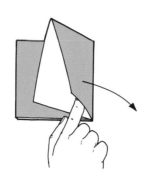

4 to open out the paper and . . .

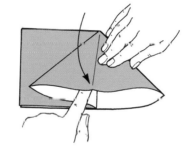

5 press it down neatly . . .

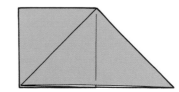

6 into a triangle.

7 Turn the paper over. Repeat steps 2 to 6 to make a waterbomb base.

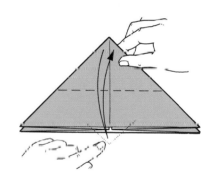

8 Fold and unfold the top point as shown.

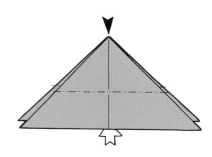

9 Sink the top point. This is what you do: Unfold the paper and flatten the top point.

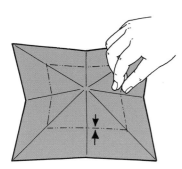

10 Crease the four sides of the inner square into mountain folds. The paper will look like a tabletop.

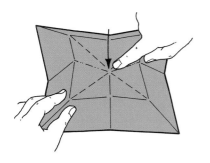

11 Push down on the middle of the square, at the same time pushing in the sides so they collapse toward the middle. Keep on . . .

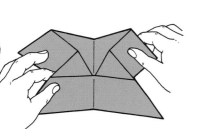

12 pushing until the square fully collapses, so inverting the point inside the waterbomb base.

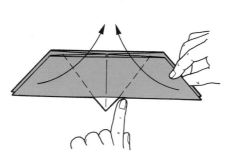

13 Here is the completed sink. Valley fold the bottom points up as shown to make the back wings.

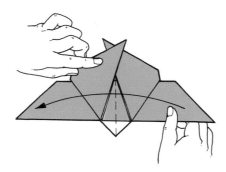

14 Valley fold the paper in half from right to left.

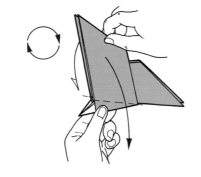

15 Turn the paper around. Valley fold the top layer of paper down on a slant as shown. Repeat behind.

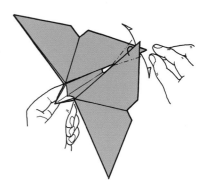

16 Open out the paper slightly. Shape the back wings with mountain folds.

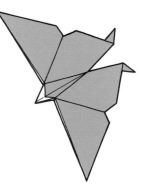

17 Here is the completed butterfly.

Figure Yakko san • **Basket** Kago

Nihonbashi has always been a bustling commercial center where old and new ways mix. Nihonbashi and its famous balustraded bridge sat at the heart of the city of Edo. The old post road to Kyoto, known as the Tokaido, began there. Kyoto was the western capital where the emperor and court lived before 1868.

Morning View of Nihonbashi: A Daimyō Procession Leaving Edo
Utagawa Hiroshige, Japanese, 1797–1858
Polychrome woodblock print from the series *Fifty-three Stations of the Tokaido*
(Tokaido Gojūsan Tsugi no Uchi), 9⅛ x 13⅞ in.
Rogers Fund, 1918 JP471

FigureYakko san

This figure is thought to be one of the oldest origami models. It represents a person who carried a decorative spear at the head of the Shogun's parade. Until 1867, the Shogun was the powerful commander of the Japanese army. When the four corners of a square piece of paper have been folded into the middle, paperfolders say that the paper has been blintzed. Blintz is the Yiddish word for a thin rolled and folded pancake. Origami enthusiasts from New York began referring to this base as a blintz during the 1950s.

Use a square piece of paper, white side up.

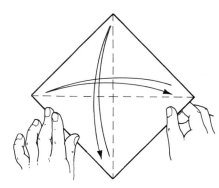

1 Valley fold the square's opposite corners together in turn to mark the diagonal fold lines, then open up again.

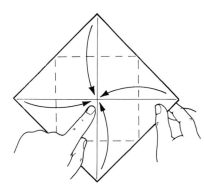

2 Valley fold the corners in to the middle, to make . . .

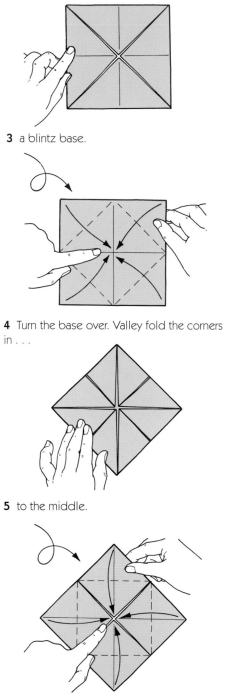

3 a blintz base.

4 Turn the base over. Valley fold the corners in . . .

5 to the middle.

6 Turn the paper over. Once again, valley fold the corners in . . .

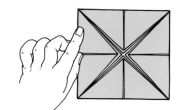

7 to the middle.

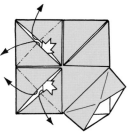

8 Turn the paper over. Open out the bottom right-hand square and . . .

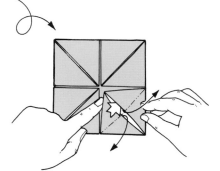

9 press it down neatly into a rectangle. Repeat with the top and bottom left-hand squares.

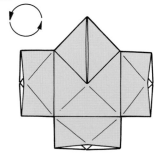

10 To complete the figure, turn the paper around.

Basket Kago

Make this basket out of sturdy paper, and it will be an ideal container for a special gift.

Use a square piece of paper. You will also need a tube of glue.

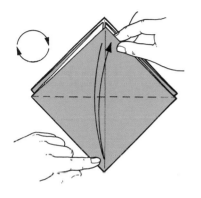

1 Begin with a preliminary fold (see page 42), white side up. Turn it around so that the open layers are pointing away from you. Fold and unfold the front flap of paper in half from top to bottom.

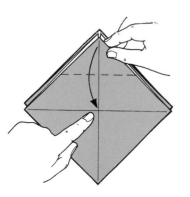

2 Valley fold the flap's tip in to the middle.

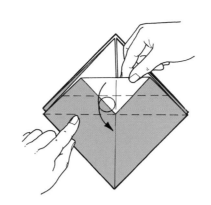

3 Valley fold the folded edge down to the middle and then over along the middle.

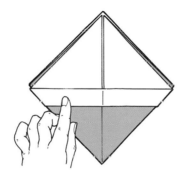

4 This should be the result.

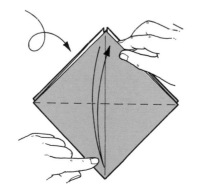

5 Turn the paper over. Repeat steps 1 to 4 with the front flap of paper.

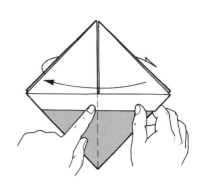

6 Valley fold the right-hand point over to the left, as though turning the page of a book. Repeat behind.

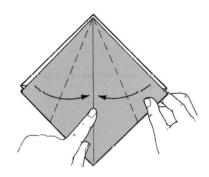

7 Valley fold the upper sloping edges over so they lie along the middle fold line.

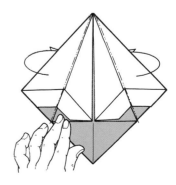

8 Repeat step 7 behind.

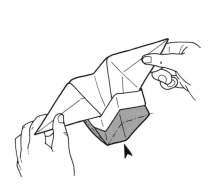

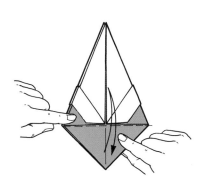

9 Fold and unfold the bottom point as shown.

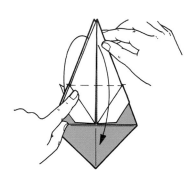

10 Valley fold the front flap of paper down as shown. Repeat behind.

11 Pinch the flaps and . . .

12 gently pull them apart. The paper will open out.

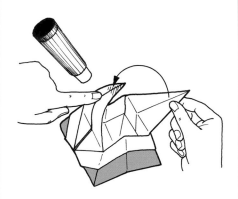

13 To make the handle, glue the flaps together as shown.

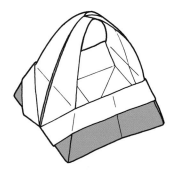

14 Here is the completed basket.

New Year Decorations and Tablewares
Ryūryūkyo Shinsai, Japanese, mid-18th–early 19th century
New Year card, *surimono* woodblock print
H.O. Havemeyer Collection, Bequest of Mrs. H. O.
Havemeyer, 1929   JP2028

初春ハ
雑煮とあらさ
ひりうるの
子のゆうある
豊洲館
四方真顔
真郡
南鄱挽ろか
菊とてきハ
うりゆわる
かきまる
かきまる
南鄱菴の
歯ろくめそ苑

Wooden Stand Sanbō
Chopstick Wrapper Hashi zutsumi

New Year's is Japan's most important holiday. In between outings to temples and
shrines, every household entertains a steady stream of visitors—relatives and friends—who
are fed special foods prepared days in advance. Children often receive gifts of money, called *otoshidama,* from the adults.
The festivities last for several days. Before Japan switched to the Gregorian calendar in the nineteenth century,
the New Year came in the spring, a time of renewal for all things in nature.

Wooden Stand
Sanbō

This origami model makes a perfect desk container for small stationery items like paper clips and pencils.

Use a square piece of paper, white side up.

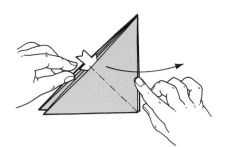

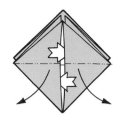

3 Lift the top half up along the middle fold line. Open out the paper and . . .

6 Open out the front square and . . .

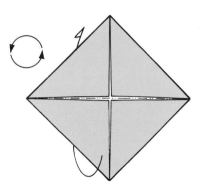

1 Begin with a blintz base (see page 48). Turn the base around to look like a diamond. Mountain fold it in half from bottom to top.

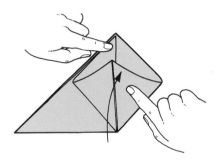

4 press it down neatly into a diamond.

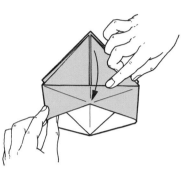

7 press it down neatly . . .

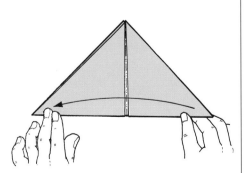

2 Valley fold the paper in half from right to left.

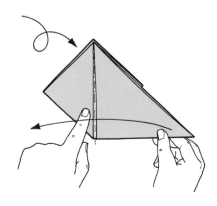

5 Turn the paper over. Repeat steps 2 to 4: You are making an upside-down preliminary fold.

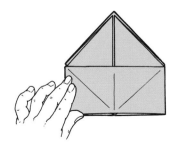

8 into a rectangle.

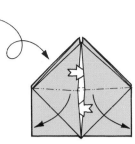

9 Turn the paper over. Repeat steps 6 to 8.

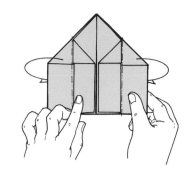

12 Repeat step 11 behind.

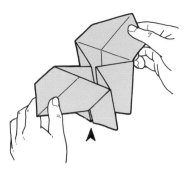

15 gently pull them apart. The paper will start . . .

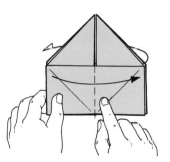

10 Valley fold the left-hand side over to the right, as though turning the page of a book. Repeat behind.

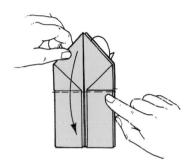

13 Valley fold the front flap of paper in half from top to bottom. Repeat behind.

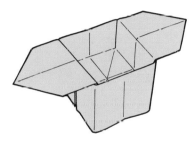

16 to open out. To make the wooden stand strong, pinch its corners and sides together.

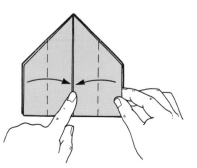

11 Valley fold the sides over to meet the middle fold line.

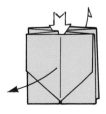

14 Pinch the flaps and . . .

Chopstick Wrapper
Hashi zutsumi

This wrapper is very easy to make, looks very decorative, and can be made in many different sizes.

Use a rectangular piece of paper, approximately 4 x 12 in. (10 x 30 cm) in size, white side up.

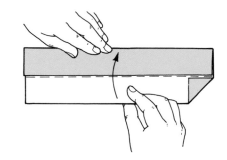

3 Valley fold the bottom edge up to meet the top edge.

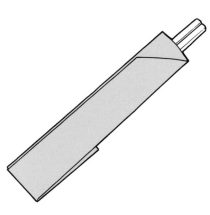

6 Here is the completed chopstick wrapper.

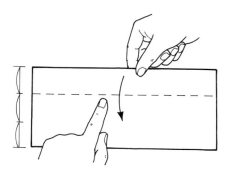

1 Place the rectangle sideways. Valley fold the top edge down one-third of the way as shown.

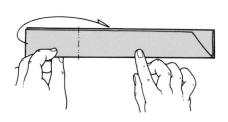

4 Mountain fold part of the left-hand side behind.

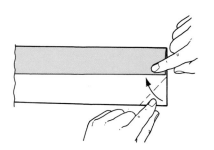

2 Valley fold the bottom right-hand corner up to meet the horizontal edge.

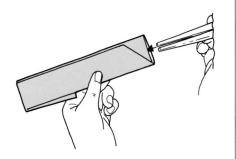

5 Insert a pair of chopsticks as shown.

Goldfish Kingyo

This small woodblock print by the artist Hokkei is printed very carefully with colors and embossing. It was probably made for a poetry club to use as a New Year's greeting.

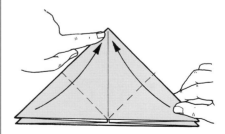

Goldfish in a Glass Bottle
Toyota Hokkei, Japanese, mid-18th–early 19th century
New Year card, *surimono* woodblock print
H. O. Havemeyer Collection, Bequest of Mrs. H. O. Havemeyer, 1929   JP2160

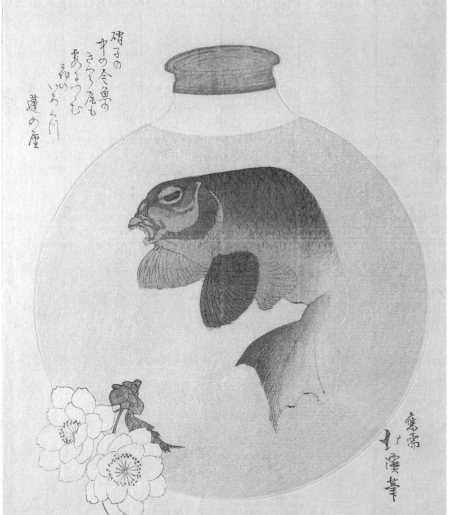

This delightful origami fold is thought to have originated in China.

Use a square piece of paper, white side up.

1 Begin with a waterbomb base (see page 45). Valley fold the bottom points up to meet the top point.

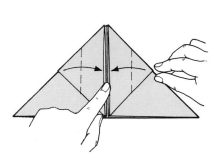

2 Valley fold the side points in to the middle.

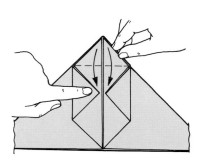

3 Valley fold the top points in to the middle to make two triangular flaps.

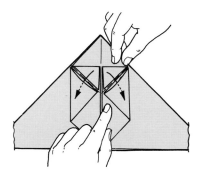

4 Tuck these flaps in to the adjacent pockets with a valley fold.

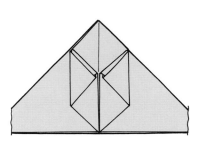

5 This should be the result.

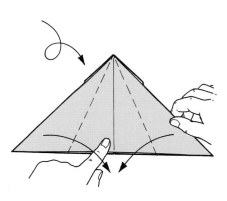

6 Turn the paper over. From the top point, valley fold the sloping edges over so they lie along the middle fold line.

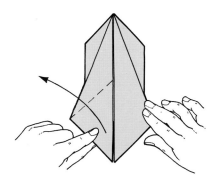

7 Valley fold the bottom left-hand point over and outward into the position shown in step 8.

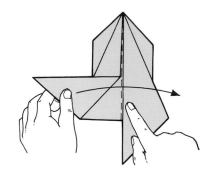

8 Valley fold the left-hand layer of paper over to the right, as though turning the page of a book.

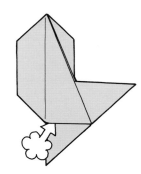

9 Hold the paper very loosely and blow gently into the small hole that you will find at the bottom. The paper will rise up . . .

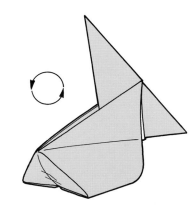

10 and form itself into the shape of a goldfish.

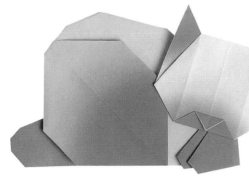

Japanese Bobtail Cat
Neko

The Torinomachi Festival can be seen here in the distance below Hiroshige's contemplative cat. It is a festival held in the weeks before New Year's at the Washi Daimyojin shrine in the heart of Tokyo's old central city. One of the favorite trinkets to be purchased at the festival stalls is a decorated bamboo rake called a *kumade*, which is just the thing to gather up all the luck and riches of the year to come. Hairpins shaped like these rakes are spread out here on the floor.

Ricefields in Asakusa on the Day of the Torinomachi Festival
Utagawa Hiroshige, Japanese, 1797–1858; 11th month of the year 1857
Polychrome woodblock print; number 101 from the series *One Hundred Famous Views of Edo (Meisho Edo Hyakkei),* 13⁷⁄₁₆ x.8⁷⁄₁₆ in., 1857
Rogers Fund, 1914   JP60

By using different shades of paper it is possible to make many different types of cat.

Use two squares of paper, both the same size and color. You will also need a pair of scissors and a tube of glue.

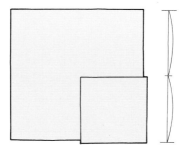

1 Begin by cutting a square of paper to the size shown. You will use this small square to fold the cat's head.

Head

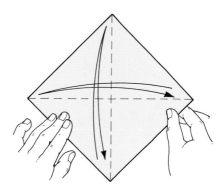

2 Valley fold the opposite corners of the head's square together in turn to mark the diagonal fold lines, with the colored side on top, then open up again.

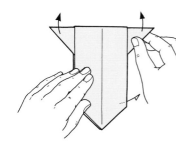

3 Valley fold the right- and left-hand corners in to meet the middle.

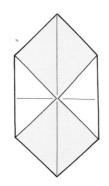

4 This should be the result.

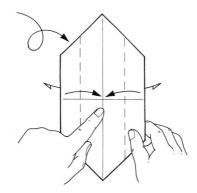

5 Turn the paper over. Valley fold the sides over to meet the middle, while at the same time letting the corners from underneath flip up.

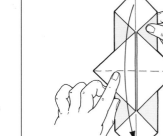

6 Valley fold the paper in half from top to bottom.

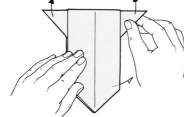

7 Pull the right- and left-hand points up as . . .

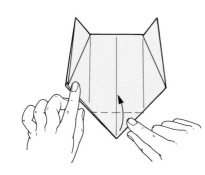

8 far as the paper will allow you, to make the ears. Valley fold the bottom points up and . . .

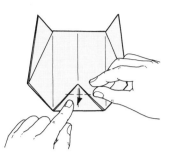

9 down again to make the nose.

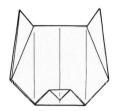

10 Here is the completed head.

Body

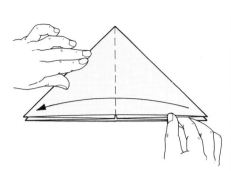

11 Begin by folding the body's square into a waterbomb base (see page 45). Valley fold the right-hand point over to the left, as though turning the page of a book.

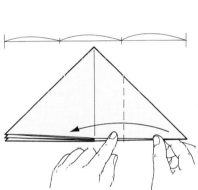

12 Valley fold the remaining right-hand point over one-third of the way to the left, and . . .

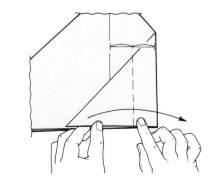

13 back out to the right as shown.

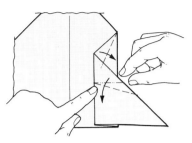

14 Open out and press down neatly the right-hand point's upper section into the position shown in step 15.

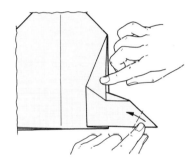

15 Valley fold the point to make the tail.

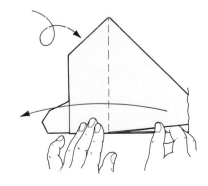

16 Turn the paper over. Valley fold the right-hand point over to the left, as though turning the page of a book.

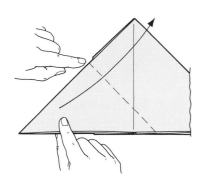

17 Noting the position of the fold line, valley fold the left-hand point over to make . . .

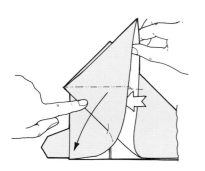

18 the bottom inside layers rise up. Open out and press the left-hand point . . .

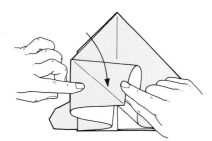

19 down neatly into a square.

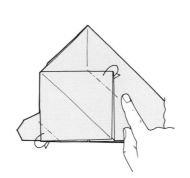

20 Mountain fold the square's top right- and bottom left-hand corners behind.

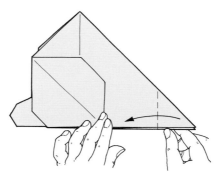

21 Valley fold the remaining right-hand points over to make the front paws.

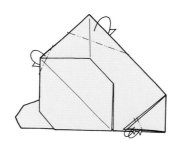

22 Shape the front paws with mountain folds. Mountain fold the top and left-hand points behind.

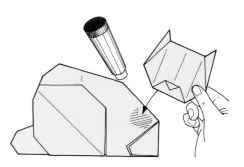

23 Glue the head on to the body at the desired angle.

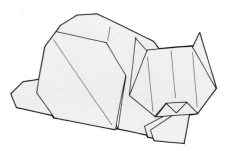

24 Here is the completed Japanese bobtail cat.

Owl Mimizuku

In Japan, many beautiful books were published in the late eighteenth and early nineteenth centuries. Poetry clubs commissioned special volumes with deluxe printing designed by the most famous artists. These books paired poetry by club members with seasonal or other natural images. The birds in this book come alive in Utamaro's sensitive drawings and make a wonderful counterpoint to the witty poems, called *kyoka,* that appear on each page.

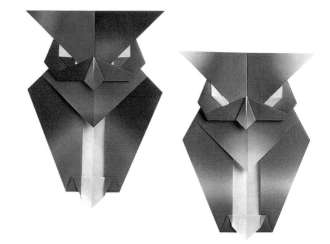

Bullfinches and Scops Owl
Kitagawa Utamaro, Japanese, 1753–1806
Polychrome woodblock print from the illustrated book *A Chorus of Birds (Momo-chidori),*
10 x 14¹³⁄₁₆ in., ca. 1790–91
Rogers Fund, 1918   Japanese Book No. 43, folio 8 recto

Try changing the angle of the eyes each time you fold this model to see how many different expressions you can give your owls.

Use two squares of paper, both the same size. You will also need a tube of glue.

Body

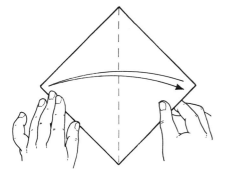

1 Turn one square around to look like a diamond, with the white side on top. Fold and unfold it in half from side to side.

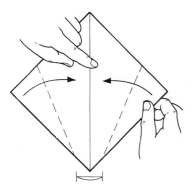

2 Starting short of the bottom point, valley fold the sloping sides over toward the middle fold line as shown.

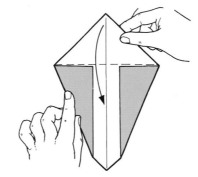

3 Valley fold the top point down on a line between the two side points.

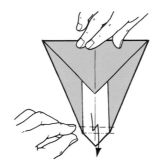

4 Step fold the bottom point.

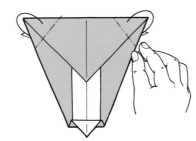

5 Mountain fold the top points behind.

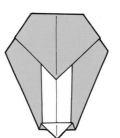

6 Here is the completed body.

Head

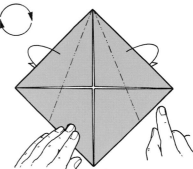

7 Begin by folding the remaining square into a blintz base (see page 48). Turn it around to look like a diamond. From the top point, mountain fold the sloping sides behind, so they lie along the middle fold line.

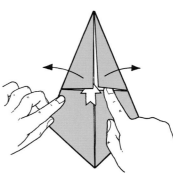

8 Unfold the two middle corners as shown.

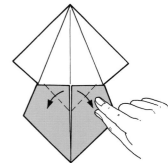

9 Valley fold the remaining middle corners out and . . .

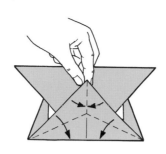

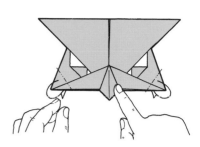

10 back in a little to make the eyes.

13 Pinch together the triangle's sloping sides, and . . .

16 To complete the head, mountain fold the bottom points behind.

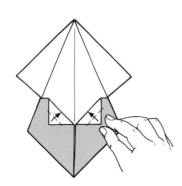

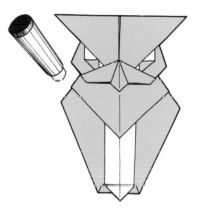

11 Valley fold the top point down as shown.

14 fold the triangular flap that appears to one side.

17 To complete the owl, glue its head on to the body at the desired angle.

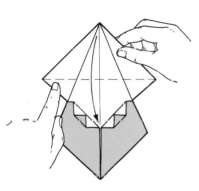

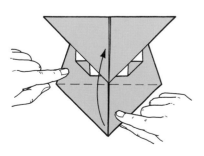

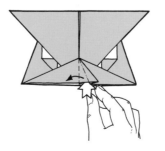

12 Valley fold the bottom point up as shown.

15 Open out the flap and press it down neatly into a diamond.

Boat Takara bune

Tokyo is crisscrossed by many canals and rivers, but the Sumida River, which rims its northeast, has a special place in the city's historical imagination. In the summer, its romantic promenades and willow-lined banks were lit by fireworks, and ferries and pleasure boats were filled with folks seeking fresh air and adventure. The site of many novels and the subject of prints and paintings, the Sumida belonged to everyone.

Ryōgoku Bridge at Evening from Onmayagashi
Katsushika Hokusai, Japanese, 1760–1849
Polychrome woodblock print from the series
Thirty-six Views of Mount Fuji (Fugaku Sanjūrokkei),
10⅛ x 14⅞ in., early 1830s
The Howard Mansfield Collection, Purchase, Rogers Fund, 1936   JP2554

This model is very popular among Japanese children, but it is comparatively unknown in the West.

Use a square piece of paper, white side up.

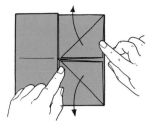

1 Begin with a blintz base (see page 48). Valley fold the top and bottom edges over to meet the middle fold line.

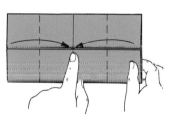

2 Valley fold the sides over to meet the middle fold line.

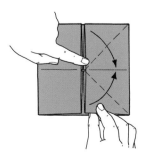

3 Valley fold the right-hand middle corners over to meet the middle fold line.

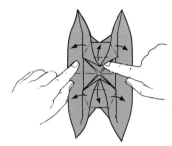

4 Pinch the middle corners and pull . . .

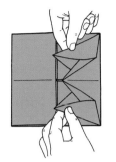

5 their outer layers apart . . .

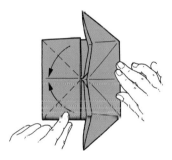

6 flattening them out as shown. Repeat steps 3 to 6 with the left-hand middle corners: You are making a windmill base.

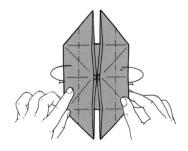

7 Mountain fold the sides behind to meet the middle fold line.

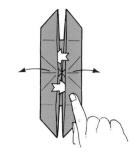

8 Open out the paper as shown to make . . .

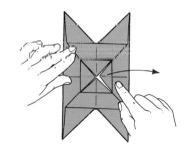

9 the inside points rise up. Flatten the folded edge of each point into the position shown in step 10.

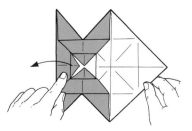

10 Pull out the right-hand middle corner.

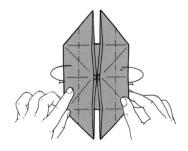

11 Repeat step 10 with the left-hand middle corner.

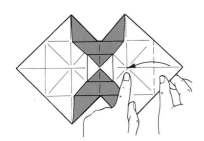

12 Valley fold the right-hand corner in as shown.

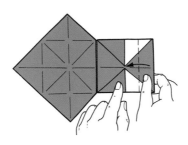

15 Valley fold the right-hand side over to meet the adjacent points.

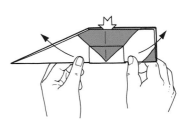

18 Careful here! Holding the paper as shown, pull gently outward . . .

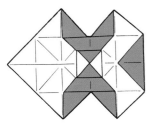

13 This should be the result.

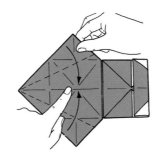

16 From the left-hand corner, valley fold the top and bottom sloping edges over so they lie along the middle fold line.

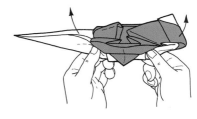

19 and upward in a half-circle, so the paper becomes three-dimensional.

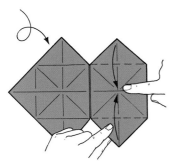

14 Turn the paper over. Valley fold the top and bottom right-hand points in as shown.

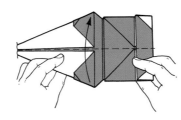

17 Valley fold the paper in half from bottom to top.

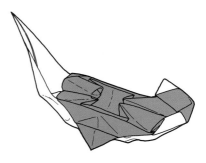

20 Here is the completed boat. The triangular flaps underneath make a perfect stand for your model.

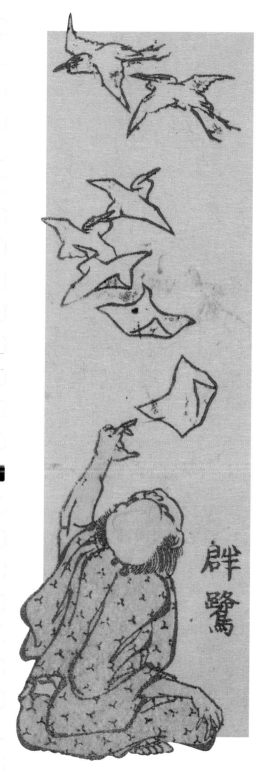

Various Magical Talents
Katsushika Hokusai,
Japanese, 1760–1849
Woodblock print from
the *Manga*, vol. X
The Howard Mansfield
Collection, Gift of
Howard Mansfield, 1936
Japanese Book No. 111,
vol. X, folio 8 recto

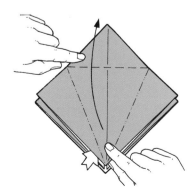

Flapping Bird Habataku tori

As an artist, Hokusai knew the magic of transformation that can be found in painting and drawing. The magician on this page of his *Manga* sketchbook could very well be the artist himself bringing paper to life.

Along with the frog and fish bases, the bird base is one of the best-known classic origami bases. Who created this magical piece of origami remains a mystery.

Use a square piece of paper, white side up.

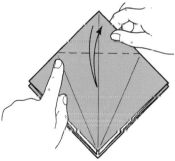

2 Fold and unfold the top point as shown.

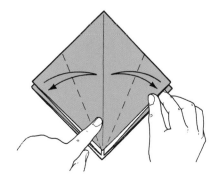

1 Begin with a preliminary fold (see page 42), white side up. Fold and unfold the lower (open) sloping edges as shown.

3 Now make a petal fold. This is what you do: Pinch and lift up the front flap of paper.

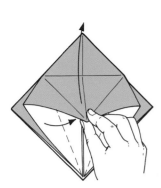

4 Continue to lift up the flap, so . . .

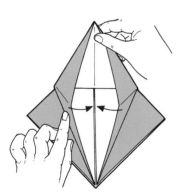

5 its edges meet in the middle.

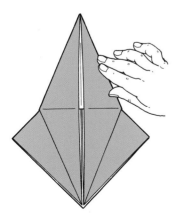

6 Press the paper flat to make it diamond-shaped. This completes the petal fold.

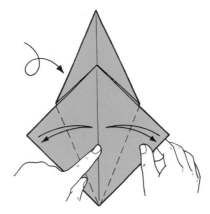

7 Turn the paper over. To make a bird base, repeat steps 1 to 6 with the lower (open) sloping edges.

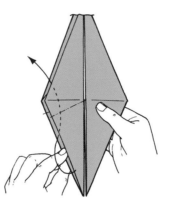

8 Inside reverse fold the bottom left-hand point into the position shown in step 9.

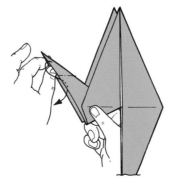

9 To make the head and beak, inside reverse fold the point's tip.

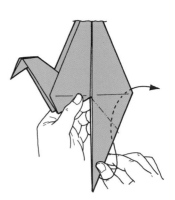

10 To make the tail, inside reverse fold the remaining bottom point into the position shown in step 11.

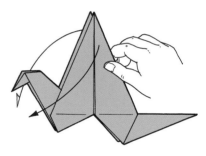

11 Curl the wings slightly to complete the flapping bird.

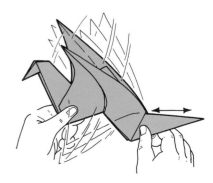

12 Hold the bird's chest, pull the tail, and the wings will flap!

Crane Tsuru

This most famous of origami folds is often used throughout the world as a symbol of peace.
If you fold a thousand cranes *(senbazuru)* within a year and string them together, it is said that they will bring you long life and good fortune. Japanese children learn origami in school to help them improve their handwriting (folding makes your fingers nimble!) and to learn about geometry. The crane is one of the most popular things to make because it uses many of the basic origami folds.

Girls Folding Paper Cranes
Japanese, 19th century
Polychrome woodblock print
Gift of Lincoln Kirstein, 1959   JP3297

Use a square piece of paper, white side up.

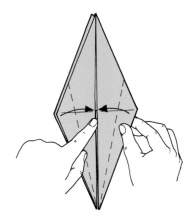

1 Begin with a bird base (see pages 67–68). Valley fold the lower sloping edges over, so . . .

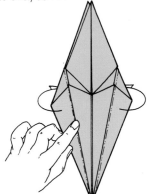

2 they lie along the middle line. Repeat behind.

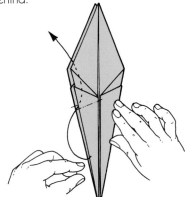

3 Inside reverse fold a bottom point.

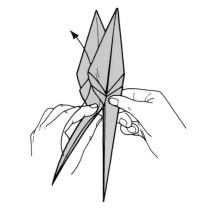

4 This shows step 3 taking place.

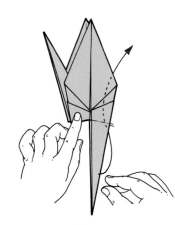

5 Inside reverse fold the remaining bottom point.

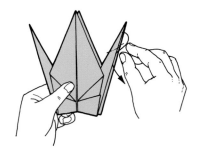

6 Inside reverse fold the tip of one of the points to make the head and beak.

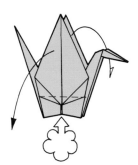

7 Pick up the paper and inflate it by blowing gently into the small hole that you will find at the bottom, at the same time pulling the wings apart and flattening out the middle point a little.

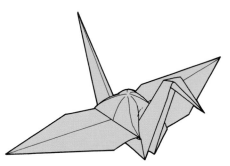

8 Here is the completed crane.

Phoenix Hōō

Many auspicious symbols came to Japan
from China, among them the phoenix.
It and three other mythical creatures
(the chimera, the giant tortoise, and the
dragon) represented the four cardinal
directions. According to lore,
the phoenix lived in
flowering paulownia trees,
ate bamboo shoots, and
drank the waters of magical springs.

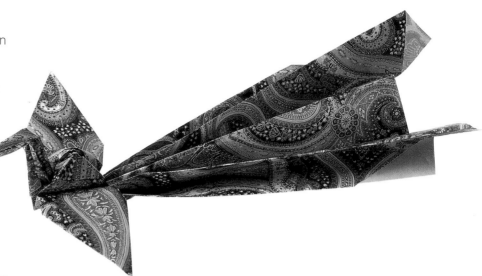

Front of Chojiya Pleasure House
Chōkōsai Eishō, Japanese, active 1793–1801
Triptych of polychrome woodblock prints, each 15 x 9¾ in., ca. 1798
The Howard Mansfield Collection, Purchase, Rogers Fund, 1936   JP2425

Even though this fold may at first appear daunting, it is very easy. As with any fold, remember to look carefully at each illustration to see what you should do.

Use a square piece of paper, colored side up.

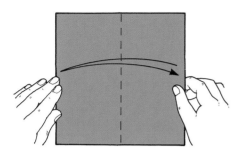

1 Fold and unfold the square in half from side to side.

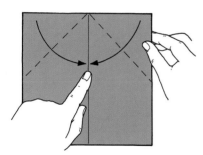

2 Valley fold the top corners down to meet . . .

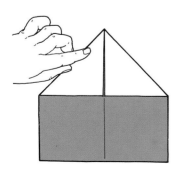

3 the middle fold line.

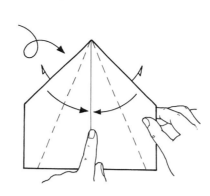

4 Turn the paper over. From the top point, valley fold the sloping edges over, so they lie along the middle fold line, while at the same time . . .

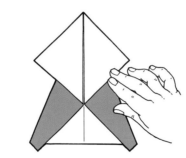

5 letting the corners from underneath flick up.

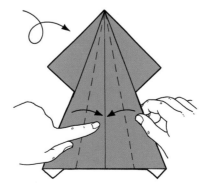

6 Turn the paper over. From the top point, valley fold the sloping edges over, so they lie along the middle fold line.

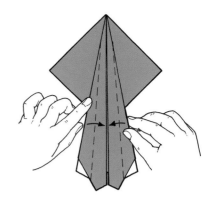

7 Starting short of the top point, valley fold the sloping edges over toward the middle line.

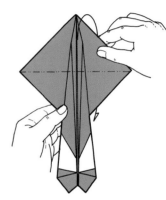

8 Mountain fold the top point behind as shown.

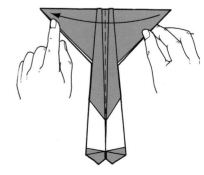

9 Valley fold the paper in half from right to left.

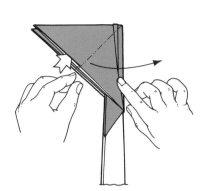

10 Lift the left-hand point up. Open it out and . . .

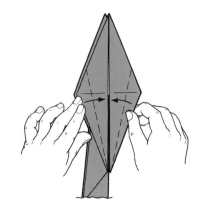

13 Valley fold the lower sloping edges over, so . . .

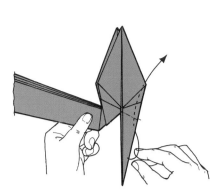

16 Inside reverse fold the bottom right-hand point into the position shown in step 17.

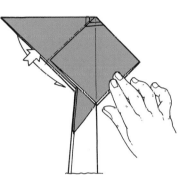

11 press it down neatly into a diamond. Repeat steps 10 and 11 behind to make a preliminary fold.

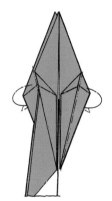

14 they lie along the middle line. Repeat behind.

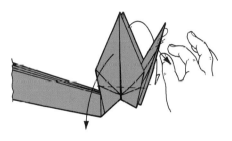

17 To make the head and beak, inside reverse fold the point's tip. Pull the wings apart and flatten out the middle point a little.

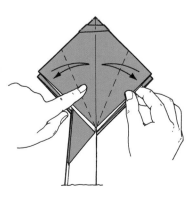

12 Repeat steps 1 to 7 of the flapping bird (see pages 67–68) to make a bird base.

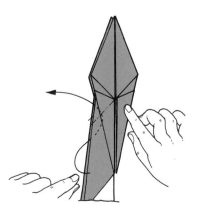

15 To make the tail, inside reverse fold the left-hand section of paper into the position shown in step 16.

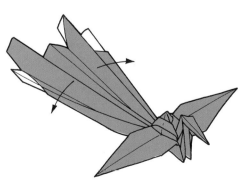

18 To complete the phoenix, open out the tail slightly.

Chrysanthemums
Utagawa Hiroshige,
Japanese, 1797–1858
Polychrome woodblock print
in fan format, 8⅗ x 11⅗ in.
H. O. Havemeyer Collection,
Bequest of Mrs. H. O.
Havemeyer, 1929 JP1899

ChrysanthemumKiku

In Japan, chrysanthemums mean autumn. They are noble flowers,
brought from China during the Nara period (710–794), and they are
used for the imperial crest. A popular Noh play titled *The Chrysanthemum
Boy (Kikujido)* tells a story of a Chinese prince who found immortality
by drinking the dew from chrysanthemum flowers.

Use two yellow squares of paper for the flower, white side up, and one green square of paper for the leaf, colored side up, all identical in size. You will also need a pair of scissors and a tube of glue.

Before you start folding: Repeat steps 13 and 14 of Lion Dance (see page 39) with each square. Use the eight small yellow squares to fold the flower. Only one small green square is required for the leaf.

Chrysanthemum

1 Begin by folding one square into a bird base (see pages 67–68). Turn the base around so that its flaps point to the right. In front, valley fold the bottom layer of paper up to the top, and behind, the top layer down to the bottom.

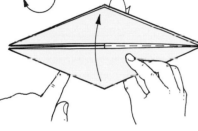

2 Valley fold the left-hand point over to the right.

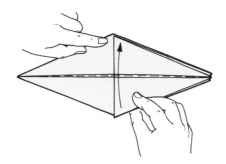

3 Valley fold the paper in half from bottom to top.

4 Valley fold the paper in half from left to right to make . . .

5 one unit of four petals. Repeat steps 1 to 5 with the remaining seven squares.

6 Glue the petal units together along their vertical edges into a circle as shown.

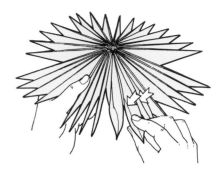

7 This should be the result. To complete the chrysanthemum, carefully open each petal out.

Leaf

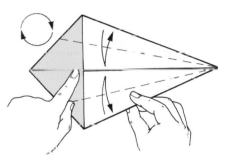

8 Begin by folding the leaf's square into a kite base (see page 34), colored side up. From the right-hand point, fold and unfold the sloping edges as shown.

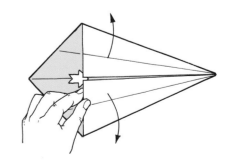

9 Unfold the kite base.

75

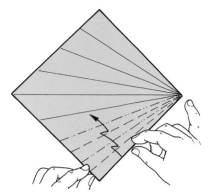

10 From the right-hand point, pleat the lower half of the paper into eight equal sections by valley and mountain folding as shown. Note that the mountain folds take place along existing fold lines.

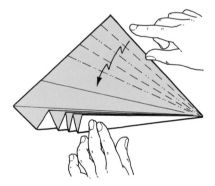

11 Repeat step 10 with the upper half.

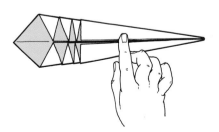

12 This should be the result.

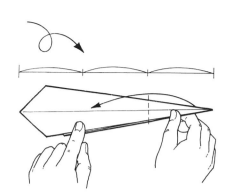

13 Turn the paper over. Valley fold the right-hand point over one-third of the way as shown.

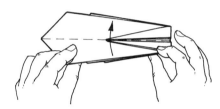

14 Valley fold the paper in half from bottom to top.

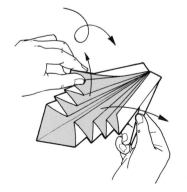

15 Turn the paper over. To shape the leaf, open out the pleats.

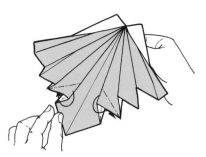

16 Reverse fold the leaf's middle pleated sections as shown.

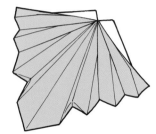

17 Here is the completed leaf.

18 Display the leaf and chrysanthemum together as shown.

Persimmon Kaki

The russet-colored persimmon is an autumn treat in Japan. In the countryside, long strings of peeled persimmon are put up to dry in the sun for winter. This set of three prints (called a triptych) shows the talent of Utamaro's printer, Tsūtaya Jusaburo. He nurtured the artist and developed spectacular technology to match Utamaro's pictorial genius.

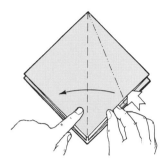

The Persimmon Gatherers
Kitagawa Utamaro, Japanese, 1753–1806
Triptych of polychrome woodblock prints, each 15 x 10 in., ca. 1805
Gift of the Estate of Samuel Isham, 1914   JP994

The tricky part of the persimmon comes toward the end when it is inflated and pulled into shape.

Use a square piece of paper, white side up.

1 Begin with a preliminary fold (see page 42), white side up. Open out . . .

2 and press down neatly into a diamond.

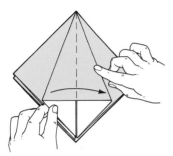

3 Valley fold the flap in half from side to side.

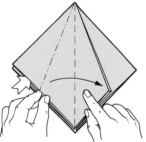

4 Repeat steps 1 to 3 with the three remaining flaps.

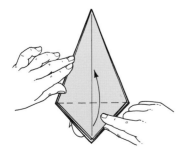

5 You should now have four layers of paper on either side. Valley fold the bottom point up as shown to make a triangle. Repeat behind.

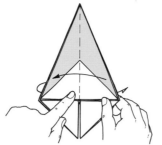

6 Find the two remaining bottom points by opening the layers of paper like pages of a book.

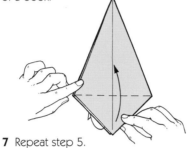

7 Repeat step 5.

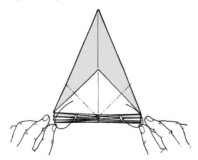

8 Mountain fold the triangle's bottom corners behind to meet the middle line to make a calyx.

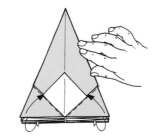

9 By opening the layers of paper like pages of a book, repeat step 8 with the three remaining triangles.

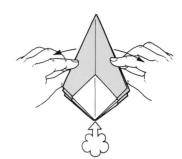

10 You should now have four layers of paper on either side. Pick up the paper and inflate it by blowing gently into the small hole that you will find at the bottom, at the same time . . .

11 pulling the layers of paper apart, and shape each calyx as shown.

12 To complete the persimmon, turn the paper over.

Frog Kaeru

The famous haiku by Matsuo Bashō (1644–1694)
on the sound of a frog unseen is one of the most lovely
meditations on tranquillity in Japanese literature:

Furuike ya
kawazu tobikomu
mizu no oto.

This pond so old;
a frog jumps in—
the sound of water.

Frog and Scarab Beetle
Kitagawa Utamaro, Japanese, 1753–1806
Polychrome woodblock prints from the illustrated book
Book of Insects (Ehon Mushi Erabi), each 10⅛ x 7¼ in., 1788
Rogers Fund, 1918   JP1057

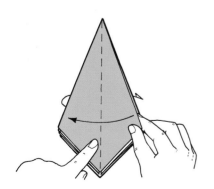

This is the model that gave its name to the frog base. The frog is a very good lesson in the technique of inside reverse folding.

Use a square piece of paper, white side up.

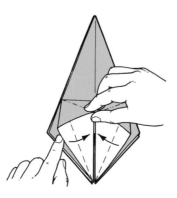

1 Begin by repeating steps 1 to 4 of the persimmon (see pages 77–78). Valley fold the front flap of paper in half from side to side. Repeat behind. You should now have four layers of paper on either side.

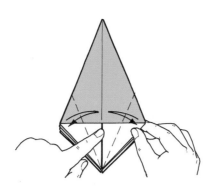

2 Fold and unfold the lower sloping edges as shown.

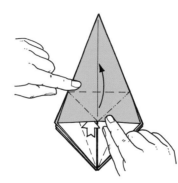

3 Pinch and lift up the flap's horizontal edge.

4 Continue to lift up the flap so its edges meet in the middle. Press the paper . . .

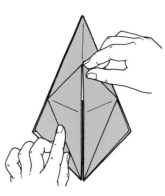

5 down neatly, making a petal fold. Repeat steps 1 to 5 with the three remaining flaps to make a frog base.

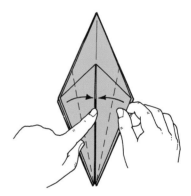

6 Valley fold the front flap's lower sloping edges over, so they lie along the middle line.

7 Repeat step 6 with the three remaining flaps.

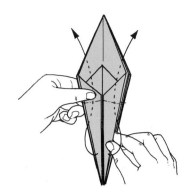

8 Inside reverse fold the two bottom points up as far as they will go to make the front legs.

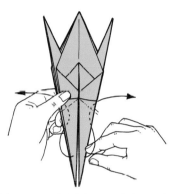

9 Inside reverse fold the remaining points out to either side to make the back legs.

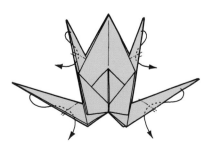

10 Inside reverse fold the front and back legs as shown.

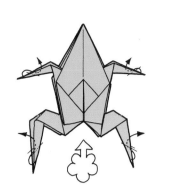

11 Inside reverse fold the tip of each leg. Finally, to make the paper inflate, blow gently into the small hole that you will find at the bottom.

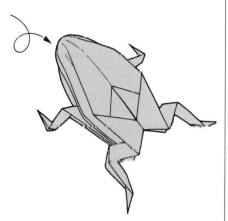

12 To complete the frog, turn the paper over. If you place the frog on a flat surface and run a finger down its back, it will jump about.

Iris Ayame

The iris appears countless times in Japanese art as a reference to the rainy time of the year, late May and June, in which it blooms in the swampy lowlands all over the country. There is a rich symbolism associated with flowers in Japanese culture, and they remain a popular subject in origami.

Irises
Katsushika Hokusai, Japanese, 1760–1849
Polychrome woodblock print from an untitled group known
as the "large-sheet flower series," 9¾ x 14⅜ in.
Frederick Charles Hewitt Fund, 1911   JP747

As we have already said, many of the traditional Japanese origami models have a symbolic meaning. This fold is no exception, as it symbolizes good health.

Use a square piece of paper, white side up.

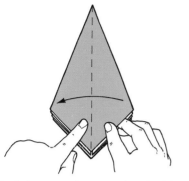

1 Begin by repeating steps 1 to 4 of the persimmon (see pages 77–78). Valley fold the front flap of paper in half from side to side.

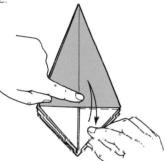

2 Fold and unfold the bottom right-hand point as shown.

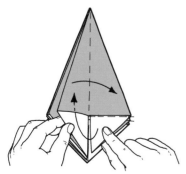

3 Return the front flap back to its original position, while at the same time inserting the bottom right-hand point underneath the adjacent layer of paper.

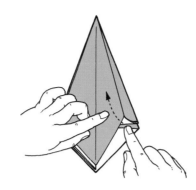

4 This shows step 3 taking place.

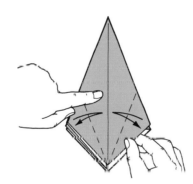

5 Fold and unfold the front flap's lower sloping edges as shown.

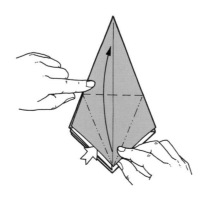

6 Pinch and lift up the front flap of paper.

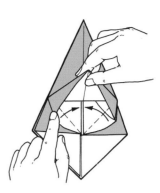

7 Continue to lift up the flap so its edges meet in the middle. Press the paper flat.

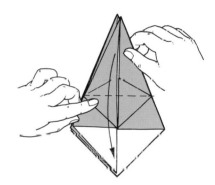

8 Valley fold the front flap down.

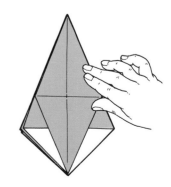

9 Repeat steps 5 to 8 with the two remaining flaps.

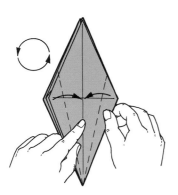

10 Turn the paper around. Valley fold the front flap's lower sloping edges over so they lie along the middle fold line.

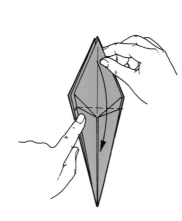

12 To make a petal, valley fold the front flap down.

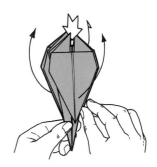

14 Lift the petals up, making the paper become three-dimensional.

11 This should be the result. Repeat step 10 with the two remaining flaps.

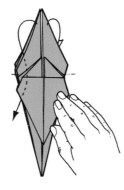

13 Repeat step 12 with the two remaining flaps.

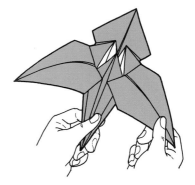

15 To complete the iris, curve the petals by rolling each one around your finger.

SnailKatatsumuri

Utamaro and his publisher, Tsūtaya Jusaburo, created some of the most beautiful woodblock prints ever made in Japan. This series, *Book of Insects (Ehon Mushi Erabi)*, was one of their most exquisite and deluxe productions. Each page pairs a naturalist's delight in the insect world with two poems rich with metaphor and observation.

Snail and Cicada
Kitagawa Utamaro, Japanese, 1753–1806
Polychrome woodblock prints from the illustrated book
Book of Insects (Ehon Mushi Erabi), each 10½ x 7¼ in., 1788
Rogers Fund, 1918   JP1055

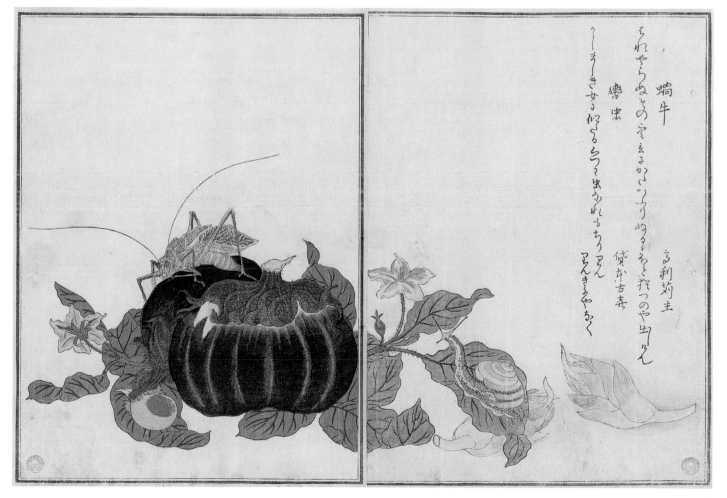

Here is a relatively easy way to make a very lifelike model. Take care when opening out the folded point during step 16.

Use a square piece of paper, white side up. You will also need a tube of glue.

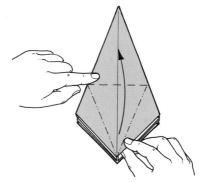

1 Begin by repeating steps 1 to 4 of the persimmon (see pages 77–78). Now repeat steps 5 to 7 of the iris (see page 83).

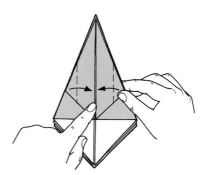

2 Valley fold the front flap's side points over toward the middle line.

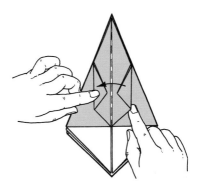

3 Valley fold the front flap of paper in half from right to left.

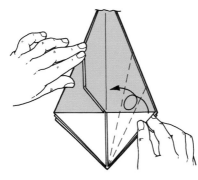

4 Valley fold the lower right-hand sloping edge over twice on its way to lie along the middle line.

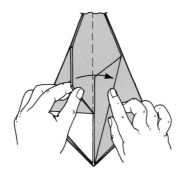

5 Valley fold the whole of the front flap over to the right.

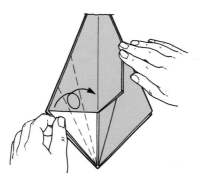

6 Repeat step 4 with the lower left-hand sloping edge.

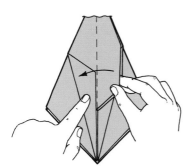

7 Return the front flap back to its original position as in step 3.

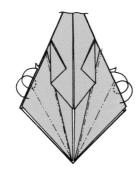

8 Mountain fold these lower sloping edges over twice on their way to lie along the middle line.

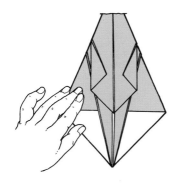

9 This should be the result.

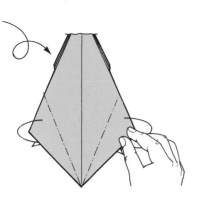

10 Turn the paper over. Mountain fold the lower sloping edges behind so that they lie along the middle line.

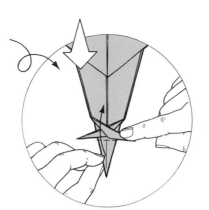

13 (the paper has been turned over) cross over each other, so making the antennae. Valley fold the bottom point up as shown.

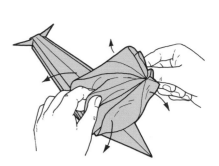

16 To make the snail's shell, open out the bottom point by pulling gently on its edges.

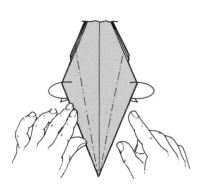

11 Repeat step 10 with these lower sloping edges.

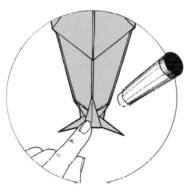

14 Glue the point down.

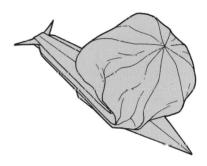

17 Here is the completed snail.

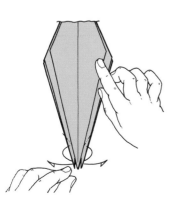

12 Valley fold the middle points out to either side so they . . .

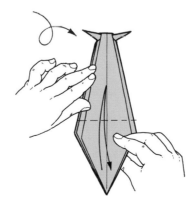

15 Turn the paper over. Valley fold the multi-layered bottom point up as far as it will go. Press it flat and unfold it.

Dragonfly Tonbo · **Bellflower** Kikyō

Tonbo, or dragonflies, flourish near water, and the rice paddies in Japan sustain many different species. They stand for the last days of summer. Dragonflies and children seem to have a special affinity, and *tonbo* are celebrated in many children's songs. In Japan, a favorite traditional toy is called a *taketonbo* or "bamboo dragonfly." It resembles a helicopter propeller and it is spun between the hands then let go to fly.

Dragonfly and Locust with Chinese Bellflower and Carnations
Kitagawa Utamaro, Japanese, 1753–1806
Polychrome woodblock prints from the illustrated book
Book of Insects (Ehon Mushi Erabi), each 10⅛ x 7¼ in., 1788
Rogers Fund, 1918 JP1051

Making this model is a very good lesson in the technique of a lovers' knot move (flattening a point). Use a square piece of paper, white side up. You will also need a pair of scissors.

Dragonfly Tonbo

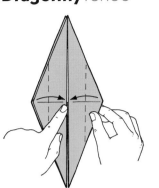

1 Begin with a bird base (see pages 67–68). Valley fold the base's side points in to the middle and . . .

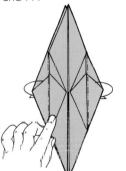

2 repeat behind.

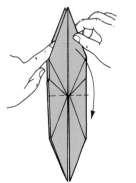

3 Pull the top flap of paper toward yourself and down in a hingelike action to make . . .

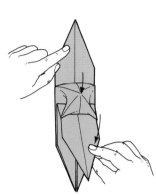

4 the middle point rise up and . . .

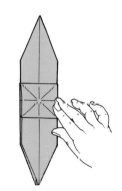

5 flatten itself down as shown. This is the lovers' knot move.

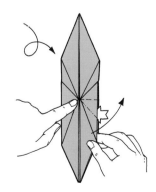

6 Turn the paper over. Lift up the bottom right-hand point. Open it out and press down neatly to the side.

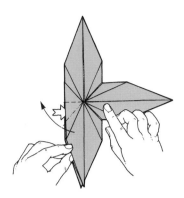

7 Lift up the bottom left-hand point. Open it out and press down neatly to the side.

8 This should be the result.

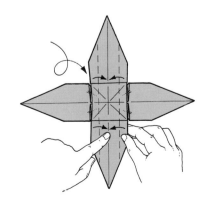

9 Turn the paper over. Valley fold the edges over to meet the middle as shown, making the . . .

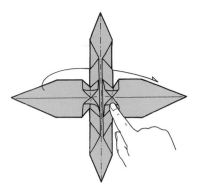

10 inside layers rise up. Flatten the folded edge of each layer as shown. Mountain fold the paper in half from left to right.

13 Open out and press down flat the head's section of paper on either side as shown, making . . .

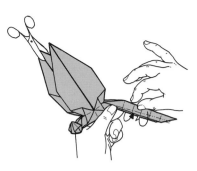

16 Shape the tail with a mountain fold. Repeat behind. Cut through both flaps as indicated to make the wings.

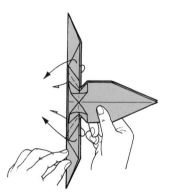

11 Outside reverse fold the top and bottom points.

14 the characteristic bulging eyes of a dragonfly.

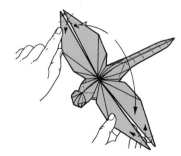

17 Open out the wings slightly and blunt their tips with inside reverse folds.

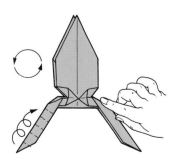

12 Turn the paper around. Roll the left-hand point up as shown to make the head.

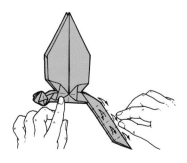

15 Fold and unfold the right point as shown to crease the tail.

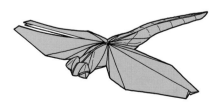

18 Here is the completed dragonfly.

Bellflower Kikyō

Many different flowers can be developed from this model. If you repeated a similar kind of folding technique, such as a reverse fold, on each of its flaps, you could well be on the way to inventing your first origami flower.

Use a square piece of paper for the flower and a smaller one for the leaf. You will also need a pair of scissors.

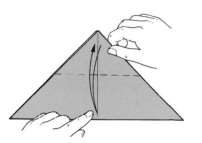

1 Begin by repeating step 1 of the dove (see page 21), with the flower's square. Fold and unfold the diaper fold in half from top to bottom.

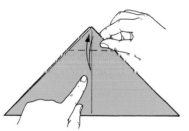

2 Fold and unfold the top point as shown.

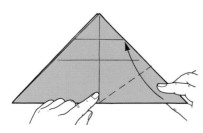

3 From the middle of the bottom edge, valley fold the bottom right-hand point over as shown.

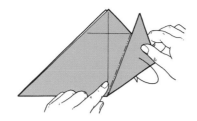

4 Again from the middle of the bottom edge, mountain fold the right-hand side behind.

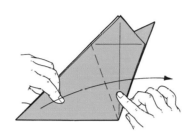

5 Valley fold the bottom left-hand point over toward the right, and . . .

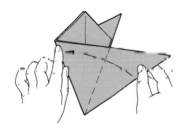

6 back to the left as shown.

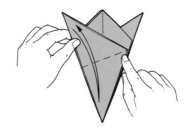

7 Fold and unfold the top left-hand point as shown.

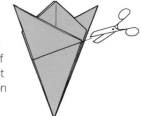

8 Cut along the indicated line. Discard the upper section of paper. Open out the lower section into a . . .

9 pentagon. Form the pentagon into a sort of preliminary fold, with the colored side on top.

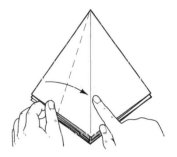

10 You should now have two layers of paper on one side and three on the other. Valley fold one flap's upper (folded) sloping edge over, so . . .

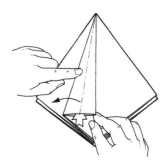

11 it lies along the middle fold line. Open out the flap and . . .

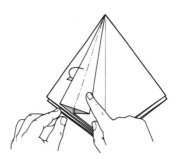

12 press it down neatly. Mountain fold the flap in half.

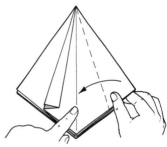

13 Repeat steps 10 to 12 with the four remaining flaps.

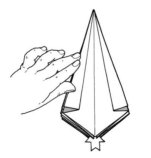

14 From the bottom, open out the paper slightly.

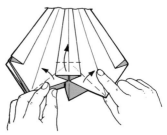

15 Valley fold a flap's horizontal edge up toward the top point as shown making . . .

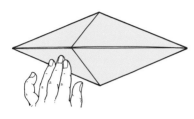

16 its adjoining layers rise up. Press them flat as shown. To make the petals, repeat with the four remaining flaps.

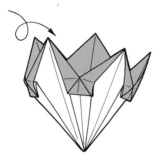

17 Turn the paper over.

18 To complete the model and give the flower its bell-like shape, curl the petals.

Leaf

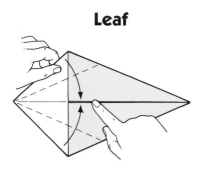

19 Begin by folding the leaf's square into a kite base (see page 34). From the base's left-hand corner, valley fold the sloping edges over . . .

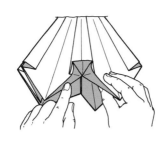

20 so they lie along the middle fold line. This completes the leaf.

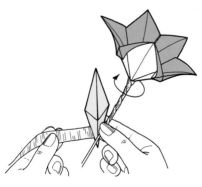

21 A TIP: To give any origami flower a stem, you will need thin florist wire and florist tape (both are available at craft stores or florist supply shops). Alternatively, you can use any thin wire and crepe-paper strips that can be wound around the wire with a little glue.

Umbrella Kasa

Sudden downpours are a part of life in Japan
and so are umbrellas. The oiled paper and
bamboo ribs of traditional umbrellas were a
picturesque addition to the urban landscape
of Edo and a favorite subject for prints and
printed book illustrations.

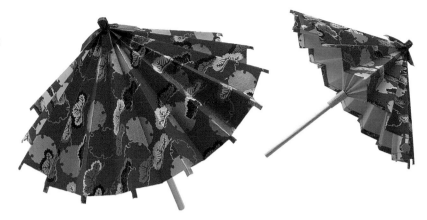

**A Shower Falls at the New Yanagi Bridge over a Canal
Joining the Sumida River**
Katsushika Hokusai, Japanese, 1760–1849
Polychrome woodblock print from *View of the Sumida River
and the Ryogoku Bridge (Ehon Sumidagawa Ryōgan Ichiran),*
7⅞ x 11¾ in., ca. 1801–1802
Rogers Fund, 1936   JP2580

Even after you have a thorough understanding of the different origami procedures and techniques, this very beautiful model will still be quite a challenge to fold!

Use two squares of paper, both the same size (try using a patterned one for the umbrella's fabric and a colored one for its frame). You will also need a pair of scissors, a tube of glue, two small rectangles of paper, a chopstick, a small square piece of paper, and some thread.

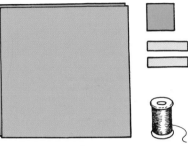

Umbrella Fabric

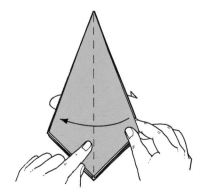

1 Begin by repeating steps 1 to 4 of the persimmon (see pages 77–78) with the fabric's square piece of paper, white side up. Valley fold the front flap of paper in half from side to side. Repeat behind.

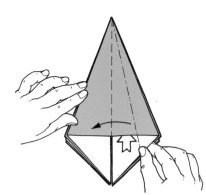

2 Open out and press down neatly one flap as shown.

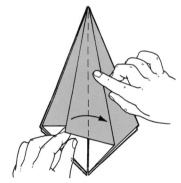

3 Valley fold the flap in half from side to side.

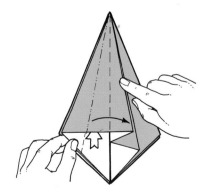

4 Repeat steps 2 and 3 with the seven remaining flaps.

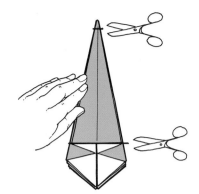

5 You should now have eight layers of paper on either side. Cut through all the layers just below the horizontal edge, then cut off the tip.

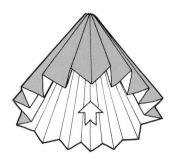

6 From the bottom, open out the paper slightly. This completes the fabric.

Frame

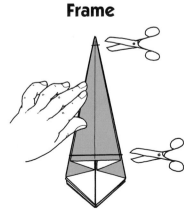

7 Begin by repeating steps 1 to 4 with the frame's square piece of paper. Cut through all the layers just above the horizontal edge, then cut off the tip.

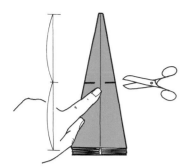

8 At the halfway point, cut a slit through all the layers at either side as shown.

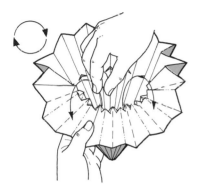

9 Careful here! Turn the paper around. Open out the paper slightly. Change the fold lines that come out from the slits from valley folds into mountain folds and vice versa, so . . .

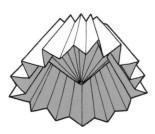

10 shaping the frame.

Assembly

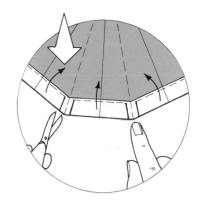

11 Glue a small rectangular piece of paper around the chopstick's pointed end.

12 Carefully tuck the frame inside the fabric as shown, and . . .

13 hold them in place by gluing around the edges.

14 This is an inside view of the fabric's edge. Make a cut on both sides of each valley fold as shown. Valley fold the edges between the cuts up . . .

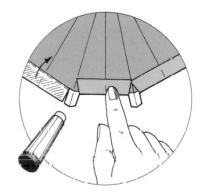

15 over the frame and glue into place.

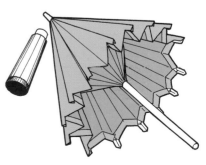

16 Insert the chopstick's pointed end through the umbrella. Glue the umbrella at its top point to the chopstick.

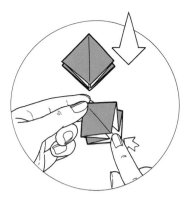

17 Fold the small square piece of paper into a preliminary fold (see page 42), white side up.

18 Glue the preliminary fold to the umbrella's top point.

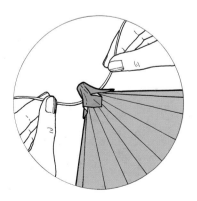

19 Tie the preliminary fold . . .

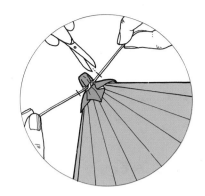

20 in place with the thread.

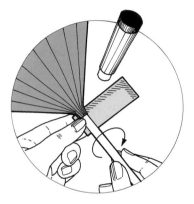

21 Glue the remaining small rectangular piece of paper to the frame's bottom point and wrap it around the chopstick as shown.

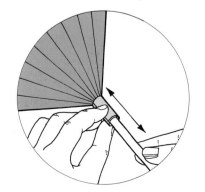

22 Make sure that the frame can pass freely up and down the chopstick.

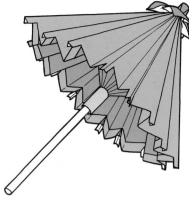

23 Here is the completed umbrella.